MAKING
BEADED
JEWELLERY

MAKING
BEADED
JEWELLERY

Over 80 beautiful designs to make and wear

BARBARA CASE

David & Charles

For my husband David

A DAVID & CHARLES BOOK

First published in the UK in 1995
First published in paperback 1998, reprinted 1998, 2000, 2003
This paperback edition published in 2003

Text, designs and diagrams copyright © Barbara Case 1995, 1998, 2003
Photography and layout copyright © David & Charles 1995, 1998, 2003

Distributed in North America
by F&W Publications, Inc.
4700 E. Galbraith Rd.
Cincinnati, OH 45236
1-800-289-0963

ISBN 0 7153 1498 X (paperback)

This book was published previously
by David & Charles as *A World of Beads*

Typeset by Ace Filmsetting Ltd., Frome, Somerset
Printed in Singapore by KHL
for David & Charles
Brunel House   Newton Abbot   Devon

David & Charles books are available from all good bookshops. In case of
difficulty, write to us at David & Charles *Direct*, PO Box 6, Newton Abbot, TQ12 2DW
quoting reference M001, or call our credit card hotline on 01626 334555.

Visit our website at www.davidandcharles.co.uk

CONTENTS

6

INTRODUCTION

What fascination beads have for us! From our earliest ancestors through to today's modern generation, beads have been a constant source of trade and adornment. For many thousands of years people have been producing beads that even now we would be pleased to own and wear. Some examples of these beautiful beads dating from as long ago as 4000BC can be seen in our museums, and a visit to The British Museum in London to look at the fascinating display of early beads will prove well worth while.

The Egyptian exhibition, in particular, demonstrates the skills of the early beadmakers, in this case at the time of the pharaohs. Some of the most ancient of manufactured beads are shown here with small, mass produced faience beads, present in great numbers. These round or tubular beads were some of the first to be glazed, most often in blue, a colour much prized by the Egyptians. They were used in large quantities for the decoration of wrappings for mummies, and also appear in the elaborate bead collars which can be seen in paintings depicting the nobility of the era. Many other beads of this time are also to be seen here with necklaces made from materials as diverse as clay, gold, and semi-precious stone. On a recent visit to this exhibition I noticed particularly one turquoise necklace, as although 4,000 years old it was made in a style that is one of my favourites today. To either end of each bead was placed a gold bead cap, with a tiny gold bead employed as a spacer between each of the larger beads. When you look through the photographs in this book you will see this design idea in use several times.

Although ancient Egypt provides some of the best early examples, beads were in fact used worldwide by all cultures, and trade in beads between many countries is known to have existed for thousands of years. In fact, some of Egypt's faience beads are thought to have originated in Crete, where a bead factory was discovered in the ruins of the famous palace of Knossos.

One of the big advances in bead manufacture came with the discovery of glass. The material was already in use for the glazing of clay and faience beads, but it was not used to make complete beads until around 1500BC. It is likely that the first glass beads were considered as valuable as those made from semi-precious stone as both types have been found together in the burial chambers of the pharaohs.

The very earliest beads, however, were probably chance finds of stone, wood or pieces of bone, which had a naturally occurring hole. Many examples of these have been found in the burial places of prehistoric man, perhaps showing that these treasures were some of his most prized possessions. It therefore seems that this early interest in beads has provided us with one of the oldest and most enduring of industries.

Over the ages, our bead making skills have gradually improved and at some time most countries have produced beads of one type or another. The Middle Ages saw the beginnings of trade in glass beads from Venice and Holland to Africa and North America, in exchange for gold, ivory, animal skins and even slaves. These particular beads have since become known as 'trade beads' and are now being rediscovered and exported as collector's pieces.

You can also 'unearth' family bead treasures; there are many old and beautiful beads lying discarded and unappreciated in attic boxes. Most beads, but especially glass or semi-precious stone, are so durable that they could last virtually for ever. For this reason, beads both ancient and modern make wonderful collector's items and can be found the world over. Enthusiasts visiting the Isles of Scilly, for instance, might like to cast an eye over the sand of Beady Pool where the remains of the bead cargo of a wrecked Venetian ship are reputed to sometimes wash ashore! I have visited this little bay and not seen any, but you may have more luck.

Finding today's beads is not difficult, as they are now available to us in an enormous range of type, colour and style. We still use beads made of stone, wood and bone, but over the thousands of years that have elapsed since the first beads were worn we have learned how to make beads from a vast range of materials and in infinite variety. Still manufactured worldwide, often by traditional methods, they are exported to and sought after by modern bead jewellery makers, and a recent upsurge in interest has created a greater demand than ever before.

My own first childhood recollection of beads is of my Grandmother's colourful jar of mixed beads and buttons with which I was allowed to play. However, it was not until much later that I started to experiment with bead jewellery making. In the early 1970s a gift of a lovely black and white daisy-chain necklace (which you can see in the photograph on page 55) provoked a desire to make more in other colours. This necklace was made from very tiny Victorian rocaille beads by an old lady in her eighties, and back in those days of flower-power it was very fashionable. It began my search for beads.

At this point I was working as a nurse so time was limited and also finding beads other than rocailles and bugles was difficult, but the lack of raw materials just made me more inventive. I discovered many ways of using small beads in jewellery from simple threading to weaving and earring making. I sought out larger beads from jumble sales, market stalls and antique shops and rapidly became hooked on the whole business of beads.

For many years my hobby gave me a great deal of pleasure and a little pin money, especially when the arrival of children put an end to full-time work. Now, in the last few years, with the children older and less demanding, I have been able to turn this interest into a more than full-time occupation, and run my own business, Bead Exclusive, supplying loose beads and accessories as well as exclusive jewellery. I find now that the more I learn about their manufacture and history, the more fascinating beads become: wherever I go, the discovery of new beads is always on my mind and visits to foreign countries offer a challenge to find native products and fresh inspiration for jewellery design. All the beads used in the designs are available from me by mail order but at the back of the book you will also find lists of other bead suppliers in the UK and around the world, together with a glossary of unfamiliar and specialist terms for beads and beading equipment.

I hope this book will allow you to catch some of my enthusiasm. Within its pages you will learn about beads and how to string them. Whether you want to restring that old broken necklace or make something special and new, you will find the instructions given here. Eventually, perhaps, the wide variety of styles and type of bead used will encourage you to stray from my designs and alter them to suit yourself. For me, the real fascination of beads is that every piece of jewellery made from them can be totally individual. After all, mass-produced jewellery can be purchased everywhere, but how much more satisfying it is to make your own unique designs from beads of known origin.

HAPPY BEADING!

EQUIPMENT AND MATERIALS

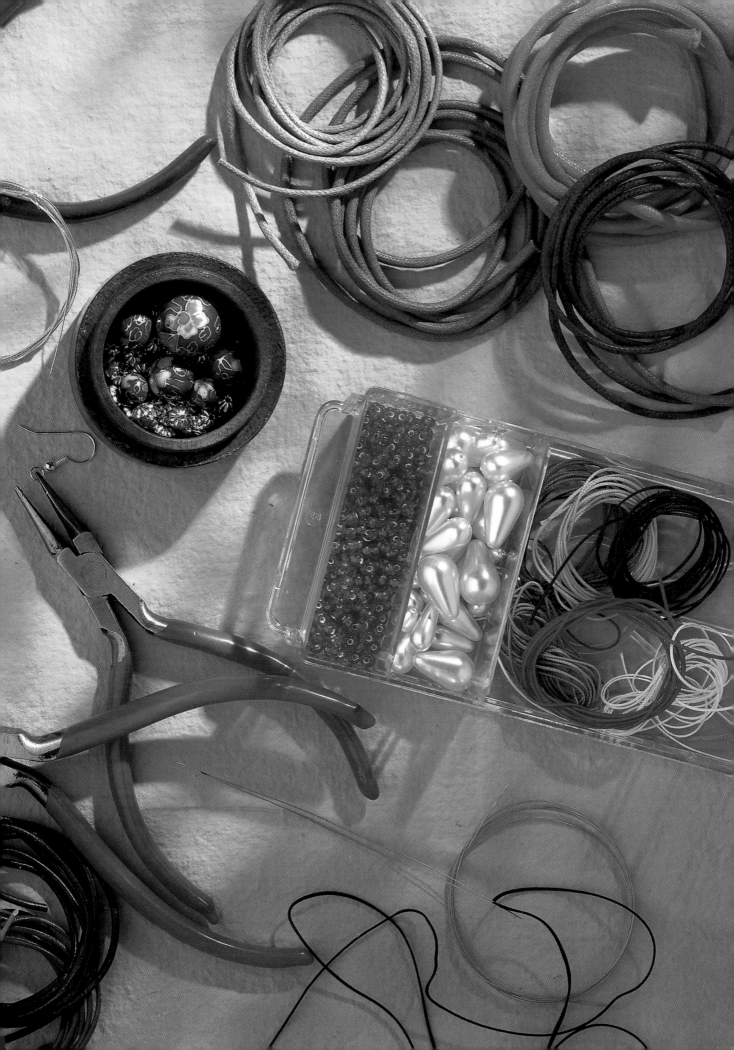

*T*he essential equipment required for making bead jewellery is not extensive and you can certainly start without needing to buy any specialist tools at all. Most of the techniques and projects in this book can be tackled using the following basic set of equipment:

• Small household pliers
• Sharp scissors
• Fine sewing needle and strong polyester sewing thread
• Gel superglue
• Shallow dish-type containers
• Household tray

As you become more involved in the craft you will gradually start to collect the purpose-made equipment which is described on pages 12–14.

• BEADS •

If you are to make bead jewellery you will obviously need to know something about beads! The following is a brief summary of the types of bead available; further details can be found in the introductions to each chapter. The first three categories are small glass beads essential to the beadworker's kit.

ROCAILLES

Rocailles are tiny glass beads made in a myriad of colours and several finishes such as silver lined, AB coated or lustred. They are cushion-shaped (flattened round) and range in size from 2mm to 5mm. In bead jewellery making they are almost indispensable both as complementary beads to their larger relations or, as you will discover in The Versatile Rocaille, as the only beads in some styles.

BUGLES

Bugles are small glass tubes which are available in a huge variety of colours and several lengths, from 2mm to 25mm. They are probably more suited to embroidery than jewellery making, but you will see them in use at least once in this book.

FILLERS

Another group of small beads are the fillers – not an exact name, maybe, but descriptive. They are larger than rocailles and produced in a more restricted range of colours. In necklace making they are invaluable, providing the filler between other more expensive beads and not only enhancing them but also reducing the total cost! Their shape varies from the traditional round to barrels, discs and roughly faceted bicones. Many are handmade; others, however, are mass produced and these can be distinguished by a tell-tale seam running along the length of the bead.

DECORATED GLASS

Decorated glass beads are available in an almost limitless range of designs and colours, and vary from cut and polished crystal to elaborate lamp beads (see Glossary). Many countries produce glass beads and the vast majority are made by hand using traditional methods. This means that even beads of the same design and colour will show slight variations in size and pattern.

PORCELAIN AND CERAMICS

Porcelain and ceramic beads are made all over the world in a huge range of types and designs, from exquisite handpainted Chinese porcelain to more roughly made clay beads from Thailand.

METAL

This is one of the largest and most varied groups of beads. I use some metal beads is nearly every piece of jewellery that I produce. They are made all over the world and vary in size and type from tiny, plain 2mm 9ct gold to huge 35mm, intricately made Indian brass spheres.

CLOISONNÉ AND ENAMEL

Cloisonné and enamel beads are a small group which, as far as I can discover, are made only in the far-eastern countries of China and Thailand. They are some of my favourites due to the fine detail, gorgeous colours and perfection of manufacture that they all exhibit. All these beads have a metal base and beautiful enamelled designs.

SEMI-PRECIOUS STONE

Beads made from semi-precious stone are more widely available today than ever before. Some are expensive, but a surprising number are much

cheaper than jewellery-shop prices would suggest. The variety of stone available is larger than you would expect, providing a range of subtle colours that are lovely on their own or blend well with any of the other categories of bead.

PEARLS

Pearls are beads with which everyone is familiar. From the real thing to the coloured-plastic imitation, they are universally popular and are available in many sizes and in a colour range from brilliant dyed hues to the natural sheen of real pearl.

BEADS FROM NATURAL SOURCES

Beads from natural sources, such as shell or seed, can be taken straight from nature and used for jewellery making with only the addition of a hole for threading. Other materials such as the exquisitely carved Chinese peach stone, Indian ebony, rosewood, horn, bone and lac (see Glossary) have been worked upon to produce some very interesting beads.

MAN-MADE MATERIALS

Beads made from plastic and other synthetic materials are not among my favourites so, with some exceptions, I do not use them for jewellery making. I know many will disagree, because the choice of colour and shape available must be unsurpassed by any other type of bead: you will find plastic beads that vary from imitation amber to pastel-coloured, delicate flower shapes, and everything in between. One of the types I do use is the Italian or American metallised plastic beads. These have all the appearance of beautiful antiqued metal but are in fact plastic beads given a metallic surface coating.

All the above categories of bead are to be found in bead shops in many countries around the world. The prices will obviously vary widely, but when you consider that the vast majority of beads are handmade you will realise that they are all relatively inexpensive.

· BEADING THREADS ·

When planning a necklace you will need to use a thread that suits your beads. There are several types of threading material from which to choose.

SILK

Silk is the traditional thread for beading. It is available in many colour variations and is often still used for threading pearls and semi-precious stone. I rarely use it, however, as I prefer to rely on the safety afforded by the strength of man-made beading threads.

POLYESTER

There are several types of polyester thread. Those that are useful in necklace making vary from ordinary strong polyester sewing thread to specialist woven-polyester beading threads, which are preferable. If you are new to beading, however, you may wish to begin a project without going to the bother of trying to find real beading thread, and in this case the sewing thread is a reasonable substitute. It is not as durable as beading thread and may eventually stretch, but if used double and with beads that are not too heavy, it should give a satisfactory result. Because this thread must be used double you will need to use a beading or very fine sewing needle when threading the beads.

Woven-polyester beading thread is the thread that I use most frequently and is recommended for the majority of projects in the book. It is made in two thicknesses: 0.06mm and 0.04mm. Where possible I use the thicker of the two as it is stronger, and unless otherwise stated this is the thread used for every project in the book. The thinner thread is, however, invaluable when making double- and triple-threaded necklaces, where some beads have to take the thickness of two or three threads.

Although these beading threads are available in many colours I nearly always use white, as in a properly threaded necklace the thread is not visible. The one exception to this is when making a knotted necklace, as in this instance the thread will be seen and should match your beads.

NYLON-COATED WIRE

Nylon-coated wire consists of fine threads of wire twisted together and covered in a thin layer of nylon. It is a little stiff to use, but is indispensable if the beads to be threaded are heavy or have sharp edges around the hole. It is also easy to use, requiring no needle or superglue and only the use of a crimp (see page 18) to attach it to a clasp.

MONOFILAMENT NYLON

Monofilament nylon is to be found in sports shops as fishing line, and personally I believe that is where it is best left. It is mentioned here only because you are likely to find it used in ready-made necklaces. Do not use it for necklace making, as it causes light beads to hang in a stiff or crooked manner, and if used with heavy beads it will stretch when warm.

LEATHER THONG

Leather thong is a good threading material to use when you wish to give an ethnic appearance to your jewellery, and is available in a variety of colours that can be co-ordinated with your choice of beads. Obviously no needle or superglue is required, but it is helpful to cut the threading end diagonally to aid its passage through your beads.

Leather thong is normally available in two thicknesses, 1mm and 2mm. All the necklaces in this book are threaded on 1mm leather – I find 2mm is too thick to pass through most beads, though it is useful for suspending a single pendant.

GLAZED COTTON CORD

Glazed cotton cord is a useful substitute for leather thong. It too is available in several colours and two thicknesses.

As with the beads, all these threading materials should be available from your bead supplier. You may also find some of them in general craft shops.

· BEADING NEEDLES ·

My preferred method of threading does not require a beading needle and instructions for it can be found in Basic Necklace Threading on pages 19–20. However, sometimes the use of a needle is necessary and you will need to choose the most suitable of the two types available.

FINE METAL

This is a very small-diameter version of a sewing needle. Although it can be used for threading, its main use is for bead embroidery or weaving on a loom. I rarely use it, due to the fine hole through which the thread must pass – it can take longer to thread one than to make the whole necklace!

TWISTED WIRE

The second type of beading 'needle' is not a true needle at all, but a length of extremely fine and pliable wire that has been twisted double to leave a fairly large and easily threaded loop. These wire 'needles' have the added advantage of flexibility, which makes them particularly suitable for threading beads such as semi-precious stones where the drilled hole is not always straight.

· BEADING TRAYS ·

Beading trays are available in several designs. The best are those which incorporate a grooved, measured section which holds the beads in order of proposed threading: this allows you to view and alter your design before making your necklace. Within the same tray are depressions that hold the smaller component parts, such as small beads and findings. This type of tray should be available from your bead supplier.

Although a purpose-made tray is ideal, you can use an ordinary household tray and lids from jars to hold the beads and components. Your beads can then be placed in order of threading in a length of card folded into an upturned W shape.

· PLIERS ·

To begin your jewellery making you may well already own a pair of small household pliers that will cope with many of the tasks required. These pliers must incorporate a cutting section, for cutting headpin wire, and as small a 'nose', or end, as possible, for bending wire. If you need to buy a pair, however, it is probably worth looking for more specialist pliers.

The three main types used for bead jewellery are: cutting pliers (for cutting wire and headpins); round-nosed pliers (for bending headpin wire into loops); flat-nosed pliers (for general use, such as opening and closing jump rings).

You should be able to buy these pliers from bead suppliers, craft shops or DIY hardware stores.

Opposite: 1 shortener clasps (pg 40); 2 crimps and calottes (pg 16); 3 spacer bars (pg 79); 4 spacers (pg 115); 5 bead caps (pg 18); 6 clasps (pg 16)

*F*indings is the general name given to the components that are necessary to complete your jewellery, such as necklace clasps and earring hooks. They are normally made from metal and many hundreds of different types are available. The ones described and illustrated here are those most commonly used, although throughout the book you will also find other, more specialist findings employed. Where this is the case, they are described and instructions given for their use. The photographs on pages 15 and 17 show all the findings mentioned here, together with variations which are used in other parts of the book.

· NECKLACE CLASPS AND FINDINGS ·

Necklace clasps are made in different styles and with great variation in quality. When choosing a clasp be careful to select one that is suitable for your beads; for example, do not use a cheap gilt-plated clasp for expensive semi-precious stones, or a lightweight 9ct gold clasp for something like heavy Indian kiln glass beads.

CLASPS

Barrel clasps are easy clasps to use, both in the making of necklaces and as a fastener for the finished necklace. They fasten by screwing the two ends together and are available in many finishes, though not usually sterling silver or 9ct gold.

Box clasps are really hook clasps in which the hook is hidden from view by a decorative 'box'. You will probably be familiar with them as the type used for most simple pearl necklaces. These are good clasps to use for delicate or valuable beads as, although dainty in appearance, the method of fastening is very secure and will not allow the necklace to fall off even if the clasp becomes partially undone. These clasps are also available in a great variety of styles and qualities, and if you require a clasp of sterling silver or 9ct gold you will probably find that there is more choice in this type of clasp than any other.

Trigger clasps are simple safety clasps that are available in several sizes and in finishes that range from plated base metals to silver and 9ct gold. They operate by a small trigger which opens the clasp and a tiny hidden spring which returns it to the closed position.

Bolt-ring clasps are likely to be familiar to everyone as traditional necklace clasps. Their method of operating is similar to the trigger clasps. They are easy to obtain and to use, but I do not choose them very often as I find the bolt mechanism is sometimes unreliable. However, this applies only to bolt-ring clasps made from plated base metals, not those in sterling silver or 9ct gold.

Jump rings or split rings must be used with both trigger and bolt-ring fasteners, providing the fastening point for the other side of the necklace. The term 'jump ring' covers many sizes and styles, but basically it means simply a ring made from metal. This may be round or oval and open or closed. Some are decorative and also useful in necklace and earring design: you can see closed oval jump rings used as spacers for the Bead Collector's necklace on page 100. Jump rings are available in plated base metals, sterling silver and 9ct gold.

Split rings are available, in base metals, in sizes from 7mm to 25mm. The smaller ones are useful as part of a necklace clasp and the latter can be used when making up keyrings.

The above are the basic necklace clasps you will require when you begin bead jewellery making. As you become more adventurous you will want to find others that particularly suit your designs. You will see other styles and types in use throughout the book and also in the photograph of findings on page 15. Most are very simple to use and the basic techniques needed are described in the next chapter. If other techniques are required, full instructions will be given with the appropriate project.

CALOTTES AND CRIMPS

To attach your clasp to the necklace you will probably need to use small findings known as calottes or crimps. I say probably, because you can often make do without these by tying your thread straight on to the clasp. This technique is described and illustrated on page 24.

*Opposite: **1** (left to right) hat pins, scotch pin, lapel pin, headpins (pg 18); **2** jump rings (see above); **3** split rings (see above); **4** earring hangers (pg 109–15); **5** sieve brooch backs (pg 52); **6** key rings (pg 87)*

Calottes are available in several styles and sizes. They are made from plated base metal, sterling silver and 9ct gold and consist of two small cups hinged together like the two sides of an unbroken cockleshell. One side of the calotte bears a loop for attachment to the necklace clasp. Their purpose is to provide a very strong and tidy finish to a necklace by covering the finishing knot and attaching directly to the clasp. You will find instructions for their use in Basic Necklace Threading on pages 19–20 and within individual projects.

Crimps are available in styles that seem to bear no relation to each other. What they do have in common is that they secure the thread to the clasp by being squeezed with a pair of pliers, to alter their shape and tighten them over the thread. Most crimps are available only in base metals.

BEAD CAPS AND NECKLACE END CAPS

Bead caps are the small and often almost insignificant plated base metal, sterling silver or 9ct gold caps that you will frequently see used either side of some beads in necklace and earring making. They vary from tiny, plain 3mm caps to quite beautiful enamel caps that look like brightly coloured flower petals. In use they enhance the appearance of the jewellery by drawing attention to some of the special beads, achieving the same sort of effect as underlining a few words in a sentence.

Necklace end caps are similar to bead caps but a more exaggerated cup shape. They are used to cover the end beads in a necklace and are particularly useful in multi-stranded necklaces, where they provide a neat finish. End caps are also useful in some earring styles.

• EARRING FINDINGS •

Like necklace findings, those for earrings are available in a huge range of styles and qualities. Those mentioned here are used regularly for the projects in this book. Any special findings are described in the projects where they are used.

EARHOOKS, POSTS AND CLIPS

Earhooks (for pierced ears) are the wire hooks that pass through the earlobe, with a loop at the bottom end for attaching the decorative part of the earring. They are sometimes known by other names such as fishhook, shepherd's crook or ball-and-spring earwires. Earhooks are available in plated base metal, sterling silver and 9ct gold, and the photograph on page 17 shows several styles.

Another commonly used earring finding is the *earpost or stud*. Like earhooks, these are used to make earrings for pierced ears and are available in plated base metals, sterling silver and 9ct gold. There are also a few hybrid earposts, in which different materials are combined in order to avoid allergy problems; for example, the post may be made from sterling silver or stainless steel and the decorative ball from a plated base metal. These findings also have a loop for the attachment of an eardrop and are useful for making earrings that are less dangly than those made with earhooks.

Clip-on earring findings are available in many styles; some clip on, some screw on and some use a combination of both fitting methods. As with all the other earring findings, they are made in plated base metals, sterling silver and 9ct gold. They are also used in the same manner, incorporating a loop from which the beaded drop hangs.

HEADPINS

For nearly all bead earrings a headpin is required to suspend a beaded drop. These pins, made in plated base metals, sterling silver and 9ct gold, are available in several lengths. For most of the earrings in this book 5cm (2in) plated headpins are used, even though in many instances they will have to be cut to a shorter length – the cost in wastage is minimal since these headpins are so inexpensive. When using more expensive sterling silver or 9ct gold, it makes sense to save money by using headpins of the correct length for the earring.

Plated headpins are also made in either hard or soft metal. The hard type are less likely to bend and spoil the appearance of the earring.

• MISCELLANEOUS FINDINGS •

Many findings do not fall into one of the previous groups. These include hatpins, brooch-backs and pins, shoe clips, hair slides, spacer bars and fancy drops for earrings. Some of these can be seen on pages 15 and 17 and are described in the projects.

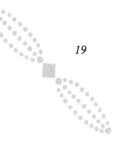

TECHNIQUES

· BASIC NECKLACE THREADING ·

*T*he technique described here is the one recommended for most of the necklaces in the book. Where necessary, specific instructions are given for individual projects. Simple necklace threading is a straightforward task but requires a little advance planning. The following items will be needed for every necklace you make:

- Beading tray, or household tray and fold of paper to hold beads (see Beading Trays on page 14)
- Shallow containers to hold small beads – jam- or pickle-jar lids are ideal
- Beads as required for your design
- 2 calottes
- 1 clasp
- Woven-polyester beading thread of the required length
- Gel and liquid superglue
- Flat-nosed pliers
- Sharp scissors

Before you start, a word of warning with regard to the use of superglue: this glue dries within seconds and is harmful to the skin. Because it bonds so quickly, it will also damage fabric or furniture and must be used with great care. Do not let children apply the glue themselves, though a ready-prepared thread is useful for youngsters to use when beading as there is no sharp needle to worry about. A release agent is available for superglue and it may be a good idea to keep some to hand.

If you feel unhappy about using superglue, then use one of the beading needles mentioned in the equipment chapter; it will make no difference to the end result.

1 Gather the beads needed for your necklace.
2 Place the larger beads, in order of threading, in the purpose-made grooved area of your beading tray or in your length of folded paper.

3 Place the small beads in the shallow containers. (If you try to put them in with the larger beads they will roll out of sight beneath them.) For ease of threading, use the shallowest containers for the smallest beads.
4 Measure out the required length of thread. The length given with each project allows for the tying of knots to the clasp – if you are making your own design, don't forget to allow an extra 15cm (6in) for this.
5 At one end of your thread, tie two overhand knots, one on top of the other. Dab the resulting knot with a small touch of gel superglue (Fig 1a). (Alternatively, you could use clear nail varnish to seal this knot.) Cut off spare thread.
6 Cover the knot with a calotte and use the pliers to squeeze it until it is closed and the thread is held securely (Figs 1b and 1c).

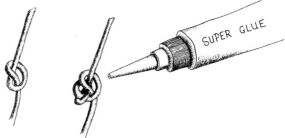

Fig 1a   Tie two overhand knots one on top of the other and apply a little gel superglue

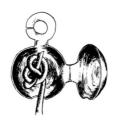

Fig 1b   Cover the knot with a calotte

Fig 1c   Close the calotte using pliers

7 Prepare the thread for threading by cutting diagonally across the other end using scissors.
8 Dip the cut end of the thread briefly into the

liquid superglue to lightly coat approximately 5cm (2in) of thread. Allow to dry.

9 When dry, the 'glued' end of the thread will become stiff enough to thread easily through the beads. Thread beads in the correct order.

10 When the threading is complete apply the second calotte, making sure that no spare thread is visible. To do this, just hold up the thread at the unfinished end and lift it to allow the weight of the beads to take up any slack (Fig 2).

Fig 2   To check that no spare thread is visible, hold up the thread at the unfinished end and allow the weight of the beads to take up the slack

11 As in step 5, tie a double overhand knot as close to the last bead as possible. Touch the knot with gel superglue and cover with a calotte (step 6).

12 The final task is to attach the clasp. Using the pliers, open either the loop on the clasp or the loop on the calotte to facilitate linking one with the other. It is better to open a loop sideways rather than outwards. This preserves its strength and makes accurate closing much easier.

ALTERNATIVE CALOTTE STYLE

The style of calotte used above is the one I prefer. However, not all bead suppliers stock it and you may come across the alternative, which is illustrated in Fig 1b for the Victorian Black Tassel necklace on page 33. They are very similar in effect and the only difference in the method of use is that with this second type you must remember to thread on the last calotte before you tie the final knot.

COVERING SPARE THREAD OR A KNOT

If your finished necklace shows a small gap of uncovered thread all is not lost! I have developed my own technique to overcome this problem and I sometimes need to use it even now. By following the instructions and diagrams you will often save yourself the work of a complete restringing. You will need:

• 1 hollow metal bead, 3mm
• Flat-nosed pliers

1 Look carefully at the 3mm bead. You will see a fine line running from top to bottom (Fig 3a). This is a seam which can be persuaded to open with gentle pressure from a pair of pliers.

2 Place the bead between the jaws of the pliers, with the jaws covering the holes and the seam facing forwards (Fig 3b).

3 Squeeze the pliers gently until the seam opens a little (Fig 3c).

4 Fit the opened bead over the spare thread and close it with pressure on the sides from the jaws of the pliers (Figs 3d and 3e).

Fig 3a   A 3mm metal bead with seam showing   *Fig 3b   Place the bead between the jaws of the pliers*

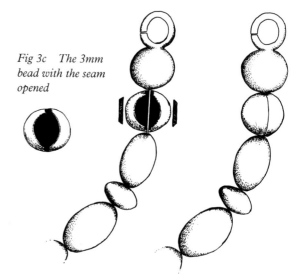

Fig 3c   The 3mm bead with the seam opened

Fig 3d   Fit the open bead over the spare thread and close it with pressure on the sides from the pliers

Fig 3e   The spare thread is now covered by the bead

· *BASIC EARRING MAKING* ·

The main skill required for bead earring making is the ability to make a loop from a headpin wire. Nearly all bead earrings will involve this technique. Although making a satisfactory loop is very simple, you will probably find that achieving a perfect loop takes some practice. The instructions below are for a simple drop earring, but can be used to make an endless variety of other earrings. All you will need to change are the beads and order of threading on the headpin. Throughout the book you will find many other designs and, where necessary, additional instructions. You will soon discover that simple earring making is very easy and in a short time you will be able to produce a pair of earrings to your own exclusive design.

As for necklace threading, collect together all the materials you will need for making your earrings:

- Household tray and several shallow containers
- Beads (as required for your design)
- 2 hard metal headpins, 5cm (2in)
- Pair of earfittings (earhooks, ball-and-post studs or clip-ons, according to preference – earhooks are used in the instructions below)
- Cutting, flat-nosed and round-nosed pliers. (You can make earrings using a single pair of household pliers. Making a perfect loop will be more difficult, but it is possible.)

1 Collect together all your beads and findings and place in shallow containers on the tray.
2 Select your beads and thread them onto the headpin (Fig 4a).
3 Use the cutting pliers to cut off any spare headpin wire. You must leave approximately 1cm (⅜in) of wire to make a loop (Fig 4b). With practice you will find that you can make a smaller and neater loop using less wire.
4 Using the flat-nosed pliers, bend the spare wire to a right angle (Fig 4c).
5 Using the round-nosed pliers, grasp the wire close to the cut end and gradually turn the pliers to form a loop in the wire (Fig 4d).
6 Attach the earring to the earfitting either by opening the loop you have just made or, preferably, the one on the fitting (Fig 4c).

Figs 4a–e *Sequence for cutting headpin wire and forming a loop*

USING LARGER-HOLED BEADS
Many beads will have a hole that is too large for the head of the headpin. In this instance your design will need to incorporate one or more smaller beads or a bead cap, which should be threaded on first to prevent the larger bead slipping off the headpin. If the bead has such a large hole that it will not sit straight on the headpin, you will also need to thread on some small rocaille or bugle beads so that they slide inside the hole of the large bead, filling the gap and holding it straight (Figs 5a–c).

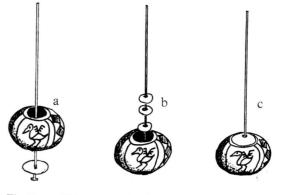

Figs 5a–c *Using rocaille beads to fill the holes of large-holed beads*

NEW FROM OLD

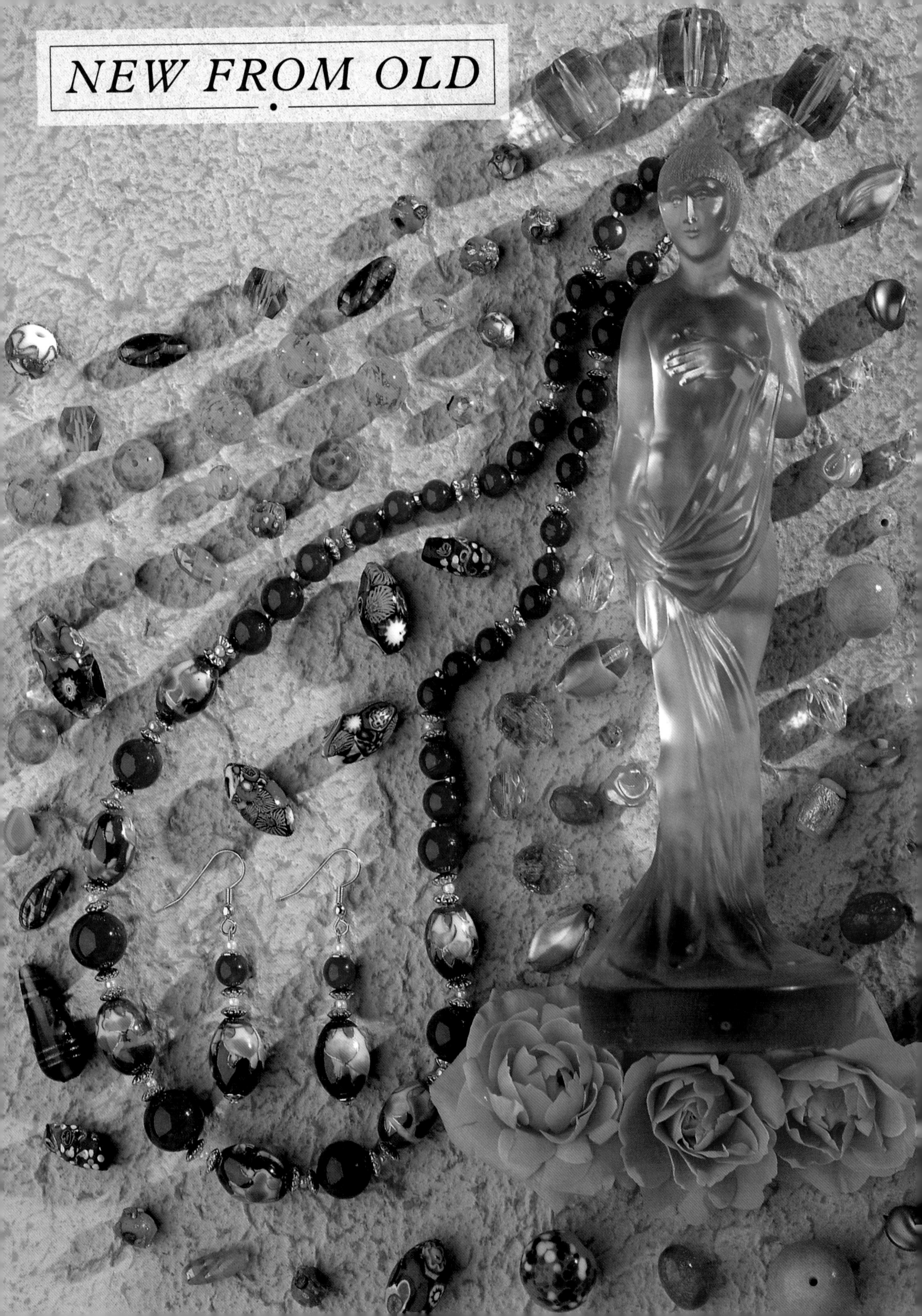

*P*ossibly one of the best ways to start beading is to rethread that old broken or unfashionable necklace. Some of my favourite beads have come from unusual sources such as bric-a-brac and market stalls, antique shops, car boot sales, charity shops, fêtes or jumble sales. One of the most likely places, though, is grandmother's old jewellery box. The results of your hunting can be very rewarding and the search itself can develop into a fascinating hobby.

I have had some special finds, among which have been Victorian jet mourning beads; beautiful pink, foiled Venetian glass; and a twisted rope of coral strung with hundreds of beads which I am still using today, ten years later!

One of the best was discovered by my daughter at a school fête, where she purchased a dirty green, broken necklace. This unlovely item turned out to consist of very old beads, probably Victorian, but most exciting of all was the clasp, not hallmarked but obviously gold. It was barrel shaped and exquisitely engraved over the whole of its surface. I decided to keep the beads and clasp together and make them into a special necklace for my daughter.

The instructions which follow show you how to clean, redesign and string an old necklace like this one using simple techniques.

CLEANING

Most old beads will need cleaning and the majority can be gently washed in a mild, soapy solution, but do not use this method for any beads of a porous nature such as wood, horn, papier mâché or some of the unglazed clays. For these, a damp cloth rubbed softly over the surface is all that can safely be tried. Other beads which are best left alone, or to expert attention, are pearls, jet and turquoise. If in doubt at all, be cautious – it would be a great pity to destroy the finish of delicate beads just for the sake of having them spotless.

Assuming you are washing your beads, beware of losing some of those precious finds down the plug hole. If they are securely strung on their original thread, leave them on this for washing. If, however, the thread seems fragile, remove the beads and wash them in an old nylon sock or stocking, with the end tied to prevent escape!

DESIGN

Most rescued beads, like those found by my daughter, will need the addition of others, old or new, either to add interest, increase length or simply replace losses. Theresa's necklace was too short and some crystal spacers were missing, so it clearly needed extra beads.

To decide on the new design I laid out the old beads in order of graduation in a bead tray. I was able to find some Chinese porcelain beads with a base colour of the same green as the old glass beads. The addition of just six of these, together with daisy-wheel beads (see Glossary) and some pink and gold rocailles, brought the 'new' necklace to a good length of 61cm (24in), and I think the result is a good example of what can be achieved, quite inexpensively, by combining old and new beads. There are so many colours and types of bead available today that you should be able to find something to match or complement any old 'treasures' that you may come across.

·*Theresa's Necklace*·

Listed below are the beads I used for this necklace, but as any old beads you may have are likely to be different you would need to change the colours. The method of tying on the clasp is very simple, so beginners can rethread their necklace without the need to buy specialist materials.

35 beads from original necklace
6 viridian-green Chinese porcelain beads, 12×18mm
40 gilt-plated daisy-wheel beads, 8mm
Packet of medium gold-coloured rocaille beads

Packet of medium pink rocaille beads
Original clasp
1 length woven-polyester beading thread or
   strong polyester sewing thread, 76cm (30in)

1 Collect together all your beads and findings and, following the photograph on page 22, place the large beads in your beading tray in order of threading. Place the small beads and findings in separate shallow containers on a tray.

2 Prepare your thread and materials using the method described in Basic Necklace Threading on pages 19–20. If using polyester sewing thread, refer to Beading Threads on pages 13 and 14 for correct use.

3 Attach the thread to the clasp using the slip knot illustrated (Figs 1a–d). For simplicity the diagram shows a single thread, but use polyester sewing thread double.

4 Touch the knot with a little gel superglue and, when dry, cut off the spare thread as close to the knot as possible.

5 Thread on the beads.

6 Take up the slack on the thread using the method described in Basic Necklace Threading on pages 19–20, and tie the other end on to the clasp following steps 2 and 3 above.

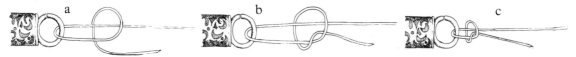

Figs 1a–c   Sequence for tying thread straight on to the clasp

· *Matching Earrings* ·

I also made matching earrings for this necklace using none of the old beads. As a feature bead I chose the Chinese porcelain and used the smaller beads as in the necklace, together with a new glass bead of almost identical colour to the old beads.

2 viridian green Chinese porcelain oval beads,
   12 × 18mm
2 green glass beads, 8mm
4 gilt-plated daisy-wheel beads, 8mm

4 gilt-plated plain bead caps, 5mm
4 small pink rocaille beads
2 gilt-plated headpins, 5cm (2in)
2 gilt-plated earhooks

1 Collect together all your beads and findings and place them in separate shallow containers on a tray.

2 To make up the earrings, follow the design in the photograph on page 22 and the instructions in Basic Earring Making on page 21.

From China come some very beautiful enamelled beads. They are always perfectly made and available in lovely glowing, transparent colours. They are formed from a base metal bead on to which the enamelled pattern is applied; any surface metal is usually plated with silver or gold. All these beads are hollow and can sometimes be very frustrating to work with, as the thread is inclined to get lost inside the bead. The only answer is patience, but don't worry – the resulting jewellery will be well worth the trouble. With such detailed and attractive beads, it is necessary to use only a few in each piece of jewellery, thereby enhancing their individual beauty.

· Chinese Choker ·

This gorgeous, simple-to-make choker uses just three Chinese enamel beads, whose rich amber colour is enhanced by the use of Indian carnelian. These carnelian beads are roughly drilled so that the holes are often of uneven size and off centre. The use of plain bead caps disguises these flaws and gives the finishing touch to the necklace. The clasp has been carefully chosen to complement the bead type and choker style.

Finished length: 45cm (17¾in)

1 Chinese enamel oval bead, 25 × 40mm
2 Chinese enamel beads, 20mm
10 Indian carnelian beads, 14mm approx
4 Indian carnelian beads, 7mm approx
2 silver-plated cushion beads, 14mm
20 Taiwanese miracle beads, 6mm (see Glossary)

6 silver-plated daisy-wheel beads, 8mm
8 silver-plated plain bead caps, 4mm
16 silver-plated plain bead caps, 7mm
1 silver-plated fancy hook clasp
2 silver-plated calottes
1 length woven-polyester beading thread, 61cm (24in)

1 Collect together all your beads and findings and, following the photograph on page 25, place the beads in your beading tray in order of threading.

2 To make up the necklace, follow the design from the photograph and the instructions in Basic Necklace Threading on pages 19–20.

· Green Choker ·

There is another example of this type of necklace photographed on the same page. Here the enamel beads chosen are a lovely emerald green and silver. To enhance their colour I have chosen a combination of green Indian glass beads, which have been given a matt finish by tumbling in abrasive grits, and green and black striped Chinese lac beads.

·Enamel Pendant with Tassel·

This necklace uses three exquisite Chinese enamel beads as 'features', with the large oval bead forming a perfect pendant that is enhanced by the proximity of the two enamel tubes of matching colour. The other small beads are chosen to complement the feature beads.
The necklace is made in a similar manner to the Victorian Black Tassel necklace on page 33, in that it uses separate threads which meet at the lower end of the pendant.

Finished length: 76cm (30in). The pendant tassel ends 10cm (4in) below this

1 Chinese enamel oval bead, 25 × 40mm
2 Chinese enamel tubes, 5 × 25mm
15 green Indian glass lozenge beads, 6 × 10mm
18 silver-plated wire beads, 5mm
1 silver-plated rose bead, 6mm
6 silver-plated beads, 3mm
4 silver-plated heishi (see Glossary)
1 packet large royal blue, silver-lined rocaille beads

12 large emerald green, silver-lined rocaille beads
1 packet medium silver-coloured rocaille beads
2 silver-plated calottes
1 silver-plated fancy hook clasp
2 lengths woven-polyester beading thread, each 61cm (24in)
1 length woven-polyester beading thread, 20cm (8in)

1 Collect together your beads and findings and place them in separate shallow containers on a tray. As nearly all the beads used in this project are small it is impractical to use a beading tray to place the beads in order of threading.

2 Following the instructions in Basic Necklace Threading on pages 19–20, prepare one of the long threads for threading and attach a calotte.

3 Following the design from the photograph on page 27, thread on the beads as far as the last blue rocaille above the largest Chinese enamel bead. Tie a spare bead loosely on to the unfinished end of thread. This is for security only, to prevent accidental loss of the beads while you are threading the other side.

4 With the second long thread, repeat steps 2 and 3. There is no need to tie on a spare bead this time.

5 Remove the spare bead from the first thread and pass both threads through a plain 3mm metal bead (Fig 1a).

6 Ensuring that the thread length is equal on both sides of the necklace, tie the threads together with an overhand knot, approximately 1cm (½in) from the 3mm bead (Fig 1b).

7 Take the third length of thread, prepare the ends for threading with liquid superglue and then thread it between the two previous threads just above the knot. Pull it to equal lengths and, using an overhand knot, tie it around one of these threads (Fig 1c).

8 Apply a little gel superglue to the knots.

9 Thread all four threads through the large oval enamel bead. (This has a large hole into which the knots will pass easily, so that they will then be covered by the bead.)

10 Thread all the threads through the next four beads, following the photograph (Fig 2).

11 Thread each of the threads through a separate heishi and then follow the sequence of beads in the photograph (Fig 2).

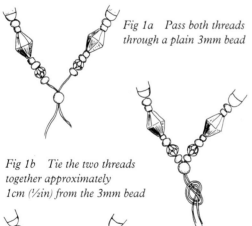

Fig 1a   Pass both threads through a plain 3mm bead

Fig 1b   Tie the two threads together approximately 1cm (½in) from the 3mm bead

Fig 1c   Thread the third thread through the first two just above the knot and tie it to one of these using an overhand knot

Fig 2   Make the tassel by threading each thread through beads as shown

12 With each thread, tie a substantial knot as close as possible to the last green rocaille.
13 Apply a little gel superglue to each of the knots.

14 Following the instructions for Basic Necklace Threading on page 20 for covering a knot or spare thread, cover each of the knots with a 3mm metal bead to give a perfect finish to the pendant tassel.

·*Enamel Bead Bracelet*·

This bracelet is made from the same type of enamel tube beads as used in the previous project and could be designed to match the pendant necklace, but here it is made from beads with black, red and white enamelling. I have chosen 4mm black faceted crystal and 3mm silver-plated metal beads to enhance the main beads. The method involves 'threading' the beads on to headpins, which are then joined together in a kind of chain. The result is a strong bracelet which should remain intact after many years of wear.

Three different pairs of pliers are included in the list of materials below. These are the ideal tools for making this bracelet but you should be able to achieve almost as good a result using a single pair of household pliers to cut and bend the headpins.

Finished length: 22cm (8½in)

4 Chinese enamel tubes, 5 × 25mm

5 black faceted-glass bicones, 4mm

10 silver-plated metal beads, 3mm

9 silver-plated headpins, 5cm (2in)

1 silver-plated barrel (screw) clasp

Cutting, flat-nosed and round-nosed pliers

or

Household pliers

1 Collect together all your beads and findings and place them in separate shallow containers on a tray. Very few beads are used in this project and many of them are small, so there is no need to use a beading tray.

2 Cut the heads off each of the nine headpins using the cutting pliers.

3 Following the instructions in Basic Earring Making on page 21, make a loop in the end of one headpin wire and attach it to the loop of one part of the barrel clasp (Fig 3a).

4 On to this headpin thread one 3mm silver-plated bead, one 4mm faceted bicone and one 3mm silver-plated bead. Cut off spare headpin wire and make a loop.

5 Make a loop in another headpin wire, attach it to the end loop of step 4 and then thread on a Chinese enamel bead. Cut off spare headpin wire and make a loop. Make a loop in another headpin wire and attach it to the end loop just made (Fig 3b).

6 Repeat steps 4 and 5 until all the beads and headpins are used.

7 Finish the bracelet by attaching the last loop made to the loop of the other part of the clasp.

a   b

Figs 3a and 3b   Joining loops to make a 'chain' of beads

·*Chinese Enamel Earrings*·

Because all the enamel beads used in the projects in this chapter are hollow they are particularly suitable for making earrings, especially if you like your earrings large but lightweight. This pair of earrings includes yet another enamel bead which, though different in design, matches the colour of the Enamel Bead Bracelet almost exactly.

2 Chinese enamel beads, 14mm

2 silver-plated metal beads, 3mm

2 silver-plated melon beads, 3 × 5mm

4 black faceted-glass bicones, 4mm

4 silver-plated daisy-wheel beads, 8mm

2 silver-plated headpins, 5cm (2in)

2 silver-plated earhooks

1 Collect together all your beads and findings and place them in separate shallow containers on a tray.

2 To make up the earrings, follow the design from the photograph on page 29 and the instructions in Basic Earring Making on page 21.

*T*here are more glass beads available than any other type, perhaps because the design possibilities really are limitless. Many countries produce glass beads, though currently the largest supplier is probably India, where the beads are often made by the farmers while they wait for their crops to grow. The income earned makes them some of the better-paid workers in the country.

· *LAMP, KILN AND FILLER BEADS* ·

Lamp beads make up the vast majority of glass beads, especially the more interesting ones. The process used for their manufacture is the same today, the world over, as it was thousands of years ago and many countries produce beads by this method, including India, Italy, Czechoslovakia, Japan and Great Britain.

I am greatly indebted to the British manufacturer Bill Tuffnell who gave his time to explain, demonstrate – and even let me try my hand at – the intricacies of lamp-bead making. The basics are as follows. A metal rod and a cane of glass are heated over a 'lamp' (jet of intensely hot flame). When the glass is glowing red and just becoming molten, the rod is dipped into a release agent (in India this is china clay, which explains the white powdery core seen inside most Indian glass beads) and the glass is wound on to the prepared end. The resulting blob of still malleable glass is taken from the heat, pressed into a mould and turned until it becomes the desired shape. This may sound easy, but I managed to get to this point only with great difficulty, and then my one bead refused to move from the rod! I did not even try the next stage, which is to decorate the bead.

One decoration technique is to 'paint' a design on to the still hot surface with trails of molten glass from smaller canes of other colours. The resulting pattern may be left raised by removing the bead from the heat at this stage, or it can be smoothed into the surface by turning in the flame for a little longer. Other options include 'feathering' the surface by pulling a sharp instrument over the decorative glass and drawing out threads of colour; covering the decoration with clear glass; inserting millefiori or rolling the semi-molten bead in granules of coloured glass to give what is known as a 'crumb' finish.

Foiled lamp beads have pieces of foil inserted beneath the top layer of glass. At their best they are very expensive, but well worth the extra cost for their glowing beauty.

One other point of interest is the use of 'goldstone' in lamp bead making, where the glass is given its sparkling quality by the introduction of tiny copper filings. You will see it in use many times throughout the book.

Kiln beads are made in a similar manner to lamp beads, the main difference being in the heat source; in this case, as the name would suggest, this is a kiln. These more roughly made beads come mainly from villages in India. Frequently the decoration is provided by the use of pieces of millefiori – glass cane which, like a stick of rock, has a picture, usually a flower, running through it. As with lamp beads, the base of the bead is wound on to a metal rod and the decoration (such as millefiori) is applied to the soft glass. The bead is then finished by reheating in the kiln to smooth the surface, before being roughly pressed into shape.

Glass *filler beads* are smaller and usually plain in colour. Some of these are made by lamp bead methods, others are mass produced (the latter can be detected by a seam running around them, obviously left by pressure from a mould). These beads are very important in jewellery making as, when carefully chosen, they do much to enhance the beauty of their bigger relations and, by spacing out the more expensive beads, help to reduce the total cost.

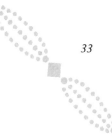

·*Victorian Black Tassel*·

The feature beads chosen for this project are very beautiful black teardrop-shaped lamp beads from India. They are fine examples of lamp beads with a decoration of raised goldstone glass, which has been applied by the 'painting' method already described. They are similar in style to some traditional Venetian beads and are among my favourites.

In this necklace only five main beads are required, with their beauty shown off by a careful choice of complementary beads and the elaborate design of the necklace. Before starting, make sure that all your beads, except the smallest rocailles, have a hole large enough to take the thickness of three pieces of thread and that the beads to be used in the top of the tassel have holes large enough to take six threads. (The thread used is of a smaller diameter than usual.)

This more complicated piece of jewellery is not difficult to make but it does take time and patience. The result is a necklace that looks good enough to become a treasured family heirloom.

Finished length: 66cm (26in). Additional length of tassel: 10cm (4in)

5 black Indian glass teardrops, 12 × 25mm
2 packets small black rocaille beads
50 medium blue/black rocaille beads
20 large gold-coloured rocaille beads
16 black glass bicone filler beads, 5 × 7mm
12 purple glass bicone filler beads, 7 × 9mm
9 purple-faceted glass discs, 8mm

18 black glass beads, 4mm
3 purple glass beads, 4mm
7 copper-coloured metal beads, 3mm
2 gilt-plated calottes
1 gilt-plated fancy box clasp
6 lengths of 0.04mm woven-polyester beading thread, each 59cm (23in)

1 Collect together all your beads and findings and place them in separate shallow containers on a tray. There are so many small beads in this necklace that it is impractical to lay the beads out in order of threading, so you must work directly from these containers.

2 Take three lengths of thread and tie them together at one end using an overhand knot (Fig 1a).

Fig 1a   Tie three threads together

3 Following the instructions in Basic Necklace Making on pages 19–20, cover the knot with a calotte (Fig 1b) and prepare the threading ends with liquid superglue. The calotte and thread should now look like Fig 1c.

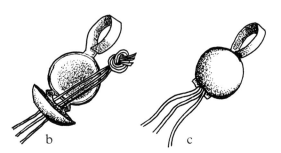

Figs 1b and 1c   Cover the knot with a calotte

4 To follow the design exactly, thread the beads on to one thread in the order illustrated in Fig 2, finishing after bead number eight on the tassel. Loosely tie a spare bead on to the thread to stop all the beads falling off while you are working with the other threads.

5 Take a second thread, pass it through the previously threaded first three beads (Fig 3) and then thread on the fifteen rocailles. Pass the thread through the next sequence of seven beads and again thread on the rocailles. Following the

order illustrated in Fig 2, continue until your thread emerges beside the first one on the tassel. Tie on a spare bead as before.

6 Using the third thread, repeat step 5. You have now completed almost half the necklace.

7 Following steps 2–5 above, make up the other side of the necklace, joining the two ends

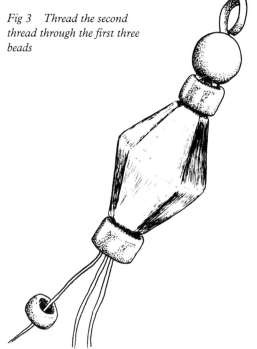

Fig 3   Thread the second thread through the first three beads

together when you thread them through the tassel beads.

8 The necklace is now almost complete and will have six threads emerging from the eighth bead on the tassel. Remove the loosely tied beads from these threads and gently pull them tight to take up any slack in the necklace. Be careful not to pull too hard or you will make the necklace stiff and it will not hang correctly.

9 Now take the six threads and tie an overhand knot as close to the bead as possible. Pull this tight and dab with gel superglue.

10 Cut off three of the threads as close to the knot as possible and, following the instructions in Basic Necklace Threading on pages 19–20, cover the knot with a 3mm metal bead.

11 With each of the three remaining threads, thread on beads in the order illustrated, finishing with a knot covered by a 3mm metal bead.

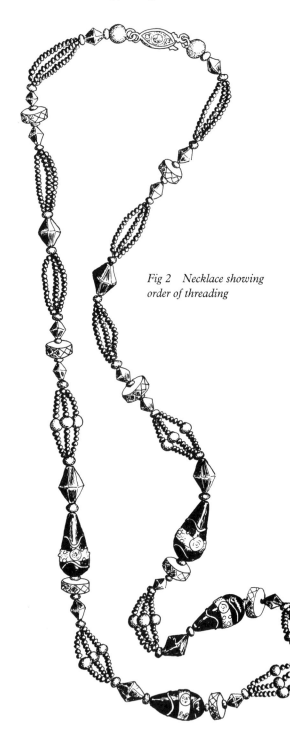

Fig 2   Necklace showing order of threading

·Smoky Glass with Pink Roses·

The feature beads of this necklace are rather special, as they were made for me by the English manufacturer mentioned in the introduction to this chapter. They are a little more expensive than many others made from glass, so the total cost has been kept down by using only five main beads. This in fact serves to emphasise their unique beauty, with the pink and green decoration on the smoky base appearing like a garland of old-fashioned roses. Others chosen to match and enhance these English beads are: Czechoslovakian glass faceted rounds in a matching smoky-quartz colour; soft-pink glass 4mm round beads; 'gold' and green rocailles; and the ever-popular 'gold' daisy wheel.

Finished length: 53cm (21in)

5 smoky-quartz glass oval lamp beads, 12 × 18mm	32 small gold-coloured rocaille beads
20 smoky-quartz faceted-glass beads, 6mm	10 gilt-plated daisy-wheel beads, 8mm
30 smoky-quartz faceted-glass beads, 4mm	2 gilt-plated calottes
16 pink glass beads, 4mm	1 gilt-plated barrel (screw) clasp
30 small green rocaille beads	1 length woven-polyester beading thread, 69cm (27in)

1 Collect together all your beads and findings and, following the photograph on page 31, place the large beads in your beading tray in order of threading. Place the small beads and findings in separate shallow containers on a tray.

2 To make up the necklace, follow the design from the photograph and the instructions in Basic Necklace Threading on pages 19–20.

·Glass-Bead Bar Brooches·

A great variety of brooches can be made simply by threading beads on to a long 'Scotch' pin. These pins are made in two lengths: 16cm (6¼in) and 13cm (5in). The method for making up is extremely simple.

Beads of your choice | Scotch pin
Small crimp (optional) | Flat-nosed pliers

1 Select your beads. The photographs accompanying this chapter will give you some ideas for how to use some of the beads already mentioned.

Fig 4a   Thread the beads on to a Scotch pin

Fig 4b   Thread on a crimp and tighten it over the pin using pliers

2 Thread them on to the Scotch pin so that the last bead sits in a position which allows for bending of the wire to form the clasp (Fig 4a).
3 The last bead should be a tight fit. If it is not, then thread on a small crimp and, using flat-nosed pliers, fasten it over the pin to hold the beads securely (Fig 4b).
4 Close to the last bead, using flat-nosed pliers, bend the wire to a right angle up towards the clasp (Fig 4c).
5 Close to the last bend in the wire, but making

sure that the point of the pin will fasten with the clasp, bend the wire again to another right angle (Fig 4d). The brooch is now complete.

Fig 4c   Bend the Scotch-pin wire to a right angle

Fig 4d   Bend the wire to another right angle up towards the clasp

·*African Look-Alike*·

The Indian glass beads used for this and the following projects are very similar to traditional African trade beads (see Glossary). They are heavy and quite roughly made kiln beads, with a large hole that would make them suitable for threading on leather. The designs shown here suit their strong colours and have been chosen to give the dramatic impact that these beads should command. In this simple-to-make necklace, the gloss of the kiln beads has a perfect foil in the accompanying frosted 10mm glass beads. The different textures give an ethnic feel without sacrificing the overall look of quality.

Finished length: 71cm (28in)

• • • • •

15 green Indian glass kiln beads,
15 × 20mm (approx)
18 green frosted-glass beads, 10mm
32 black glass disc beads, 10mm
1 packet large terracotta-coloured rocaille beads
2 gilt-plated calottes
1 metallised-plastic barrel (screw) clasp
1 length woven-polyester beading thread,
170cm (68in)
Sewing needle

• • • • •

1 Collect together all your beads and findings and, following the photograph above, place the large beads in your beading tray in order of threading. Place the small beads and findings in separate shallow containers on a tray.
2 To make up the necklace, follow the design from the photograph and the instructions in Basic Necklace Threading on pages 19–20, but use a double thread as the beads are heavy. A needle is required for threading with a double thread, but as all the beads have a large hole an ordinary sewing needle should be suitable.

·*Trade-Bead Choker*·

A few copies of African trade beads give this necklace a definite feel of a sultry continent. Combined with brass-inlaid ebony discs and bicones, they make a necklace that demands attention.
This is a very simple project, but due to the weight and sometimes rough edges of the large beads I recommend that you use nylon-coated wire for the threading.

Finished length: 46cm (18in)

4 Indian millefiori trade-bead tubes, 14 × 30mm
3 Indian millefiori trade beads, 20mm
6 Indian ebony discs with twisted brass-wire
inlay, 20mm
8 Indian ebony bicones, 6 × 12mm
20 black glass filler-bead discs, 10mm

16 large black rocaille beads
2 gilt-plated crimps
1 gilt-plated barrel (screw) clasp
1 length nylon-coated wire, 61cm (24in)
Cutting pliers and flat-nosed pliers

1 Collect together all your beads and findings and, following the photograph above, place the large beads in your beading tray in order of threading. Place the small beads and findings in separate shallow containers on a tray.

2 Attach one half of the clasp to one end of the nylon-coated wire, threading on a small crimp before threading through the loop of the clasp.

3 Now thread the wire back through the crimp, so that your clasp and wire look like Fig 5a. Leave a 5cm (2in) overlap of wire.

4 Secure the threads together close to the clasp by squeezing the crimp on to the wire using flat-nosed pliers. Make sure that the wire is held tightly by the crimp.

5 Thread on your beads in the order shown in the photograph, making sure that the spare wire from attachment of the clasp is also covered by beads (Fig 5b).

6 When all the beads have been threaded, attach your clasp by repeating steps 2 and 3.

7 Thread the left-over wire back through the beads for approx 5cm (2in) and then cut off the spare wire using pliers so that the end will be hidden by a bead.

Fig 5a   Thread the nylon-coated wire through the crimp, then through the loop of the clasp, and then back through the crimp

Fig 5b   Thread on beads to cover both wires

·Trade Beads Double Strung·

This double-strung necklace demonstrates a different design possibility using the same feature beads as in the previous project. The overall effect is changed totally by the use of companion beads which pick up the colours of the millefiori in the trade beads. The resulting bright necklace is equally at home over a winter sweater or summer teeshirt. The method for making up this necklace is similar to but simpler than that for the Victorian Black Tassel necklace (page 33) and it will be helpful to refer to those diagrams. The differences are that this necklace has only two threads and no tassel, and the threads therefore run continuously through the necklace from clasp to clasp. You could, of course, make it using three threads for the extra cost of only a few more rocailles.

Finished length: 76cm (30in)

3 Indian millefiori trade-bead tubes, 14 × 30mm
2 Indian millefiori trade beads, 20mm
10 yellow African ceramic cushion beads, 12mm (very approx)
16 green roughly faceted bicones, 6 × 10mm
22 blue roughly faceted bicones, 4 × 6mm

2 packets large dark green, silver-lined rocaille beads
2 gilt-plated calottes
1 gilt-plated barrel (screw) clasp
2 lengths woven-polyester beading thread, each 92cm (36in)

1 Collect together all your beads and findings and place them in separate shallow containers on a tray. As there are so many small beads in this design it is impractical to use a beading tray to place the beads in order of threading.

2 Following Figs 1a–c on page 33 for the Victorian Black Tassel necklace, prepare two threads for threading.

3 Following the photograph on page 39 for sequence, thread the beads on to one length of thread. Tie a spare bead loosely on to the end of the thread.

4 Pass the second thread through the first six beads.

5 Thread on nine rocaille beads to match the beads on the first thread.

6 Pass the thread through the sequence of the five beads which follow the rocailles on the first thread.

7 Continue threading in this manner, with nine rocaille beads threaded on between every sequence of larger beads through which both threads pass.

8 When the second thread is complete, untie the spare bead from the first thread. Pull the two threads to equal lengths and tie them together as close as possible to the last bead, using an overhand knot.

9 Apply a little gel superglue to the knot, cut off the spare thread and cover the knot with a calotte, following the instructions in Basic Necklace Threading on page 20.

10 Attach the clasp to the calottes.

·Long Necklace Using Necklace-Shortener Clasp·

This long necklace is extremely simple to make but is one of the most versatile of all designs as its style varies according to the way it is worn. It may be worn double, triple, knotted, or twisted and fastened with the necklace-shortener clasp. Look at page 41 and you will see it photographed in several different guises.

The necklace is made in one continuous length without a clasp and works very well with simple, plain beads such as pearls or black glass, but a very different and attractive finish is achieved by using beads of varying sizes and types. You can see the effects of the use of different beads in the photograph.

Finished length: 178cm (70in)

252 glass melon beads, 4 × 6mm
42 gilt-plated metal beads, 3mm
1 packet medium matching rocaille beads

1 gilt-plated necklace-shortener clasp
1 length woven-polyester beading thread, 193cm (76in)

1 Collect together all your beads and findings and place them in separate shallow containers on a tray, from which you will work directly.

2 Tie a spare bead loosely on to one end of the thread.

3 Following the instructions in Basic Necklace Threading on pages 19–20, prepare the threading end with liquid superglue.

4 Thread on all the beads, with a rocaille between each melon bead and a 3mm metal bead after every sixth melon bead. Do not thread on the last 3mm metal bead.

5 The two ends of the thread must now be joined together. Remove the first bead that you

tied on loosely and then, with the necklace suspended by the two loose ends (don't drop them!), tie an overhand knot as close as possible to the beads.

6 Apply gel superglue to this knot and cut off the spare thread. To give a perfect finish and make the knot undetectable, cover it with the last 3mm metal bead, following the instructions in Basic Necklace Threading on pages 19–20.

CLOISONNÉ GLORY

Cloisonné beads are exquisite examples of Chinese metal beads. They are made on a copper or brass base on to which fine wire is soldered to form a pattern of little enclosures, or cloisonnés. These cloisonnés, with usually at least one flower depicted, are enamelled in several colours with a separate firing for each. The bead is then polished and the cloisonné wire gilded.

The most striking bead of this type is the relief cloisonné in which only the flowers and so on are enamelled and the background colour is gold plated.

This very pretty bead can be seen in the photograph on page 45.

Another interesting bead is made by combining cloisonné with cinnabar (see Glossary). Here the cloisonné work is applied in a band around the bead and the cinnabar added later. When hardened the cinnabar is carved, creating a very unusual and obviously fairly expensive bead. You will see several examples of it in use through the book, especially in the Oriental Cinnabar and Lac chapter.

·*Cloisonné and Glass 'Jet'*·

This beautiful necklace is very simple to make. The only skills you will need are threading and using calottes for fastening the clasp. I have used black cloisonné and black glass jet, but both these beads are available in other colours and you may wish to try a different combination.

Finished length: 61cm (24in)

1 black cloisonné bead, 20mm
2 each black cloisonné beads, 18mm, 14mm and 12mm
4 black cloisonné beads, 10mm
6 each black faceted-glass beads, 12mm and 10mm
6 black faceted-glass teardrops, 6 × 10mm
2 black glass beads, 8mm
4 black glass beads, 6mm
6 black glass beads, 4mm
22 gilt-plated daisy-wheel beads, 8mm
1 packet large dark green rocaille beads
2 gilt-plated calottes
1 fancy gilt-plated box clasp
1 length woven-polyester beading thread, 80cm (31in)

1 Collect together all your beads and findings and, following the photograph on page 42, place the large beads in your beading tray in order of threading. Place the small beads and findings in separate shallow containers on a tray.

2 To make up the necklace, follow the design from the photograph and the instructions in Basic Necklace Threading on pages 19–20.

·Black Cloisonné and 'Jet' Earrings·

The earrings in the photograph on page 42 feature the same large beads as the necklace in the previous project. The style is altered slightly by the use of bead caps and different gilt-plated beads. Although these earrings look large, they are not heavy to wear, as all cloisonné beads are hollow. They are simple to make and involve only simple threading and loop making, as described in Basic Earring Making on page 21.

2 black cloisonné beads, 20mm
2 black faceted-glass teardrops, 6 × 10mm
2 black glass beads, 4mm
2 gilt-plated metal beads, 3mm

2 gilt-plated metal bicones, 5mm
4 fancy gilt-plated bead caps, 8mm
2 gilt-plated headpins, 5cm (2in)
2 gilt-plated earhooks

1 Collect together all your beads and findings and place them in separate shallow containers on a tray.

2 To make up the earrings, follow the design from the photograph on page 42 and the instructions in Basic Earring Making on page 21.

·White Cloisonné Choker·

As a complete contrast to the previous project, this necklace uses the same type of beads in a different colour and used in a bolder style. This particular batch of cloisonné beads is very interesting, as the colouring of the flowers varies so much. If you study the photograph on page 42 you will see that no two beads are the same, though they all have the white base colour and the greens of the leaves also match. The 10mm frosted-glass beads in two greens match the leaves and provide the link between the large cloisonné beads.
The large cloisonné beads are not threaded right up to the clasp, for two reasons: one, large beads at the back of the neck do not allow the necklace to 'sit' correctly, and two, when situated close to a clasp they make fastening it very difficult.
This necklace is one of the simplest and quickest in the book to make, and even a complete beginner should be able to complete this project within about forty-five minutes.

Finished length: 48cm (19in)

11 white cloisonné beads, 20mm
8 dark green frosted-glass beads, 10mm
8 light green frosted-glass beads, 10mm
22 gilt-plated daisy-wheel beads, 8mm
6 small gold-coloured rocaille beads

2 gilt-plated calottes
1 gilt-plated barrel (screw) clasp
1 length woven-polyester beading thread, 63cm (25in)

1 Collect together all your beads and findings and, following the photograph on page 42, place

the large cloisonné and frosted-glass beads in your beading tray in order of threading. Place the small beads and findings in separate shallow containers on a tray.

2 To make up the necklace, follow the design from the photograph and the instructions described in Basic Necklace Threading on pages 19–20.

·*Cloisonné Hat- or Lapel Pin*·

Another very easy project, this hatpin only requires the simple threading of beads and possibly the use of a crimp to hold the beads in place.
The beads are a combination of those used in the White Cloisonné Choker with a few extras included to give added interest.

1 white cloisonné bead, 20mm
1 dark green frosted-glass bead, 10mm
2 gilt-plated daisy-wheel beads, 8mm
2 gilt-plated metal bicones, 5mm
1 large silver-lined dark green rocaille bead

1 gilt-plated metal bead, 3mm
1 gilt-plated hatpin, 13cm (5in)
1 gilt-plated hatpin protector
1 gilt-plated crimp (optional)
Flat-nosed pliers

1 Collect together all your beads and findings and place them in separate shallow containers on a tray.

2 Following the photograph below, for sequence, thread the beads on to the hatpin.

3 Try to ensure that the last 3mm bead is a very tight fit on the hatpin. (The hole size will vary from bead to bead so you may need to try several.) If you cannot find one that is a good fit, then thread on a small gilt-plated crimp and, making sure that it sits closely against the last bead, squeeze it using pliers so that it will not move on the hatpin wire and secures the beads in place.

The classic string of pearls must be the most popular necklace in the western world. It would be wonderful if we could all afford some of the real thing, but for most of us the nearest we will get to this is the freshwater or Biwa pearl. In recent years these have become less and less expensive due to their culture in China. They are small, irregular, rice-shaped and are available in several colours, natural or dyed. The quality also varies greatly, those with the brightest lustre having the greatest value.

There are several substitutes for the traditional pearl. There is, of course, the cultured variety – again expensive – or the more accessible imitation. These may be made from glass or plastic. The latter may be dyed to almost any colour imaginable and are thus very useful, but I prefer to use glass as the weight gives a more genuine feel.

In this chapter I have tried to provide you with lots of fresh ideas for the use of pearls. You will find necklaces, earrings, brooches, and even hatpins – all designed to make you look at the beautiful pearl in a new light!

·*All Dressed Up*·

This wonderful triple-strung necklace (with matching earring set) is time-consuming to make, but the end result will bring the wearer many compliments. The beads used are glass pearls which impart a lovely weight and feel to the finished piece.

Finished length: 68cm (27in)

263 glass pearls, 4mm
28 glass pearls, 10mm
56 fancy gilt-plated bead caps, 6mm
2 gilt-plated calottes

1 gilt-plated fancy box clasp
3 lengths 0.04mm woven-polyester beading
  thread, 1m (39in)

1 Collect together all your pearls, bead caps and findings and place them in separate shallow containers on a tray. As this is a triple-strung necklace it is neither practical nor useful to lay the beads out in order of threading in a bead tray, but far better to work directly from the containers.

2 Following Figs 1a–c for the Victorian Black Tassel necklace on page 33, prepare the three lengths of thread and attach a calotte.

3 Thread one thread through four 4mm beads (beginning and end of necklace only).

4 Thread on a bead cap, one 10mm pearl and one more bead cap.

5 Thread on three 4mm pearls, followed by the sequence above.

6 Continue threading in this order until all the 10mm pearls have been used. Finish with four 4mm pearls.

7 Take a second thread and pass it through the first 4mm pearl.

8 Now thread on three 4mm pearls.

9 Pass the thread through the bead caps and 10mm pearl.

10 Continue this sequence to the end of the necklace.

11 Using the third thread, follow steps 7–10 (Fig 1).

12 The necklace is almost complete, but you will now need to adjust the tension on the three threads to make them all equal. Do this by gently pulling and easing until you can see that the pearls in the necklace are hanging evenly.

13 Tie an overhand knot as close as possible to the last pearl, cover with a calotte and attach the clasp.

Fig 1   Threading the third thread

·*All Dressed Up Earrings*·

These matching earrings are simple to make, requiring only the skill of bending headpin wires into loops.

2 glass pearls, 10mm
20 glass pearls, 4mm
4 gilt-plated fancy bead caps, 6mm

8 gilt-plated headpins, 5cm (2in)
2 gilt-plated earhooks

1 Collect together all your beads and findings and place them in separate shallow containers on a tray.

2 Thread three 4mm pearls on to three separate headpins. Cut off the spare wire and make a loop in each.

3 Cut the head off a fourth headpin and make a slightly larger loop than normally used for earring making.

4 Before closing this loop, attach the three beaded headpins from step 2 (Fig 2).

5 On to this fourth headpin thread one bead cap, one 10mm pearl, one bead cap and one 4mm pearl. Cut off the spare wire, make a loop and attach to the earhook.

Fig 2   Hang beaded headpins on to the loop in the fourth headpin

·Amber Teardrop·

An 'amber' glass embroidery stone (teardrop shape with a flat back) provides the focus for this unusual pearl evening necklace. These embroidery stones are available in many colours and shapes, but this faceted 'amber' teardrop seemed to be just right for the style of this necklace. It has a hole top and bottom which allows it to become the feature of the necklace by providing the link between the two strands of pearls. The round faceted-glass beads were chosen for their colour, which matches that of the teardrop. The pearls are my favourite creamy glass and have a lovely deep sheen. They would blend well with many other colours and you could make the same style of necklace with colours chosen to co-ordinate perfectly with your special evening dress.

When making up this necklace, follow the photograph on page 46. Remember also that between every large bead there is a small gold-coloured rocaille. The only exception to this is at the centre of the necklace, where the threads pass through the jump rings of the faceted teardrop with just a 6mm pearl on either side.

Finished length: 56cm (22in)

90 glass pearls, 6mm
2 glass pearls, 4mm
1 amber faceted-glass teardrop embroidery stone, 10 × 30mm
16 amber faceted-glass beads, 4mm
8 gilt-plated hogan beads, 8mm (see Glossary)
1 packet small gold-coloured rocaille beads

2 jump rings
2 gilt-plated calottes
1 gilt-plated fancy box clasp
1 length woven-polyester beading thread, 66cm (26in)
1 length woven-polyester beading thread, 86cm (34in)

1 Collect together all your beads and findings and place them in separate shallow containers on a tray. With two strands of thread and so many small beads it is easier to work directly from these than to use a beading tray.

2 The faceted teardrop stone has a hole top and bottom. To enable you to use it for this necklace, open and affix a jump ring to each of these holes (Fig 3).

Fig 3   Affix a jump ring to each hole in the teardrop

3 Prepare the two threads for threading following the instructions in Basic Necklace Threading on pages 19–20.

4 Put the other two ends of the threads together and join them by tying an overhand knot.

5 Apply a little gel superglue to the knot and, after cutting off any spare thread, cover with a calotte.

6 Pass both threads through one gold-coloured rocaille and one 6mm pearl. Continue with alternate beads until you have threaded on nine pearls, finishing with a rocaille.

7 Pass both threads through one gilt-plated hogan bead. The two threads now divide. To identify them, we will call the short thread A and the long thread B (Fig 4).

8 Thread A through beads in the following sequence: one rocaille, one 4mm pearl, one rocaille, one 6mm pearl, one rocaille, one 6mm pearl, one rocaille, one 6mm pearl, one rocaille, and one 4mm faceted bead. Omitting the first

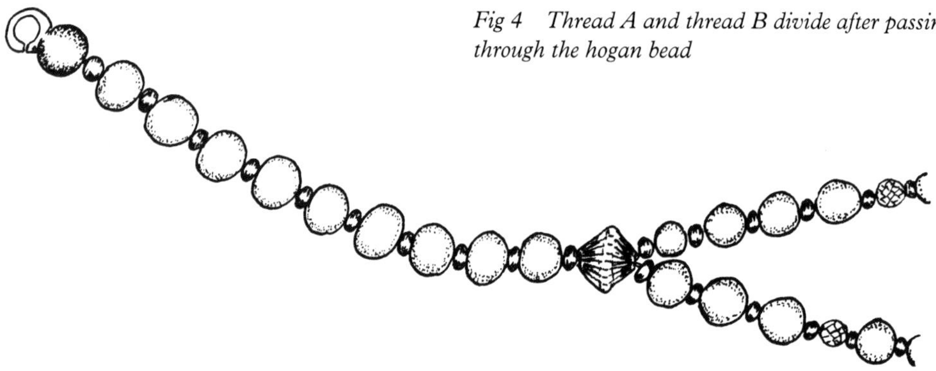

Fig 4   Thread A and thread B divide after passing through the hogan bead

rocaille and 4mm pearl, repeat this sequence three times more, then once more but replacing the 4mm faceted bead with a hogan. Thread on one 6mm pearl. Now thread through the top jump ring of the faceted teardrop and thread on the whole sequence in reverse order. Tie a spare bead loosely to this thread.

9 Thread B through beads in the following sequence: one rocaille, one 6mm pearl, one rocaille, continue until three pearls are threaded, followed by one 4mm faceted bead. Repeat, using four 6mm pearls, and then one 4mm faceted bead. Repeat, but thread on one hogan in the centre of the pattern. Repeat the four-pearl sequence, without the central hogan, twice more. Thread on a hogan instead of the last faceted bead. Thread on one 6mm pearl and then pass the thread through the lower jump ring

of the faceted teardrop. Now follow the above sequence in reverse order.

10 Thread B now rejoins thread A. Copying the start of the necklace, again in reverse order, thread it up through the hogan, the nine pearls and the rocaille.

11 The two threads now emerge together at the last bead. Gently ease them to pull in any slack thread, but be careful not to overtighten or you will destroy the graceful effect of the necklace by making it hang stiffly.

12 Remove the spare bead from thread A and, following steps 4 and 5 tie an overhand knot with both threads, apply gel superglue and cover the knot with a calotte.

13 Complete the necklace by attaching the clasp, following the instructions in Basic Necklace Threading on pages 19–20.

·*A Pearl For All Seasons*·

This very simple-to-make necklace needs no special skills, just those explained in Basic Necklace Threading on pages 19–20. However, by combining pearls with Indian glass the resulting necklace is unusual in that it is suitable for wear all the year round and at any time of day. It is also far removed from the 'twinset and pearls' image that so often deters the young from wearing a pearl necklace. The Indian beads chosen for this project are black and each has different-coloured millefiori flowers. They are enhanced by the use of gilt-plated fancy bead caps and tiny gold-coloured rocaille between each bead. The appearance of this necklace could be changed completely by using other 12mm accompanying beads.

Finished length: 79cm (31in)

42 glass pearls, 12mm
13 black Indian glass millefiori beads, 12mm
1 packet small gold-coloured rocaille beads
26 gilt-plated fancy bead caps, 8mm

2 gilt-plated calottes
1 gilt-plated barrel (screw) clasp
1 length woven-polyester beading thread,
94cm (37in)

1 Collect together all your pearls and millefiori beads and, following the photograph below, place them in your beading tray in order of threading. Place your rocaille beads and findings in separate shallow containers on a tray.

2 To make up the necklace, follow the design from the photograph and the instructions in Basic Necklace Threading on pages 19–20.

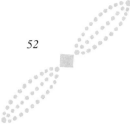

· Pearl Cascade ·

Pearls are the main beads used in this brooch, with a variety of others added to give extra interest. You could adapt the style and use different colours and types of bead to make a piece of jewellery which will meet your exact requirements. A sieve brooch-back provides the base for this versatile design, which can also be pinned to a bow to make a very dressy hair ornament.

To make this brooch exactly as shown, follow the photograph below where the order of threading can be seen clearly. The instructions given below are for this brooch, but can be adapted for use with other beads.

This project is a little more complicated than some of the others in the book, but with a little patience even a complete beginner should be able to achieve a satisfactory result.

Finished length: 13cm (5in)

2 each glass pearls, 12mm and 10mm
10 glass pearls, 8mm
17 glass pearls, 6mm
8 glass pearls, 4mm
3 gilt-plated filigree beads, 10mm
1 pale clear-brown plastic drop, 10 × 40mm
1 gilt-plated filigree cone (to fit above)
5 amber Taiwanese miracle beads, 6mm
4 each brown faceted-glass beads, 6mm
and 4mm
2 gilt-plated wire beads, 4mm

35 gilt-plated metal beads, 3mm
16 very small gold-coloured rocaille beads
1 gilt-plated metal bead, 4mm
1 gilt-plated metal teardrop, 6 × 10mm
4 gilt-plated fancy bead caps, 8mm
1 sieve brooch-back, 30 × 20mm (see photograph on page 52)
5 gilt-plated headpins, 5cm (2in)
1 length woven-polyester beading thread, 91cm (36in)

1 Collect together all your beads and findings and place them in separate shallow containers on a tray.

2 Prepare one end of the thread for threading with liquid superglue.

3 Tie a double knot in the other end and apply a little gel superglue.

4 From the back of the sieve, thread through a hole at one side, so that the knot is at the back (Fig 5a).

5 Thread through one pearl and a small rocaille, then thread back through the pearl and the same hole on the sieve (Fig 5b).

6 Continue threading pearls and rocailles in this manner, using a separate hole in the sieve for each, until much of the top of the sieve is covered in pearls (Fig 5c).

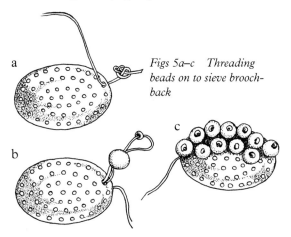

Figs 5a–c   Threading beads on to sieve brooch-back

7 Now thread on enough pearls and other beads to make a loop of the length you require. (This brooch has two loops; one uses 18cm (7in) of thread, the other 13cm (5in).)

8 Pass the thread back through another vacant hole on the sieve.

9 Repeat steps 7 and 8, making another loop, either longer or shorter than the first. Hold the sieve up and make sure that these two loops hang well together. Tie a spare bead loosely on to the thread at the back of the sieve.

10 Make two headpin drops of different lengths, following Fig 6, making sure that when attached to the lower end of the sieve they will hang just below the two beaded loops (see photograph). Attach these two drops to the sieve in a position where they will present a balanced appearance.

11 The brooch is almost complete. Hold it up and check for gaps through which the sieve back can be seen, untie the loose bead from the thread and fill any gaps by threading on more beads as in step 5.

Fig 6   Two headpin drops for the cascade, showing threading sequence

12 When you are satisfied with the appearance of the brooch, finish off by tying a knot close to the back of the sieve and applying a little gel superglue to it. Cut off any spare thread.

13 Now take the brooch-back, fit it to the sieve and secure it by closing the four tabs tightly over the front of the sieve using pliers (Fig 7).

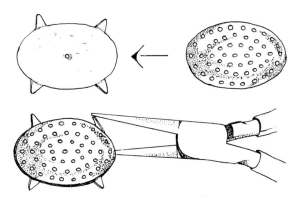

Fig 7   Fit the sieve into the brooch-back and close the tabs over the sieve using pliers

·*Pearl Hat- or Lapel Pin*·

The final project of this chapter is very simple and requires no special skills at all. The resulting piece of jewellery can be worn as originally intended – as a hatpin – or, more commonly nowadays, as a lapel pin. This particular style is delicate and reminiscent of days gone by.

1 glass pearl, 10mm
1 glass pearl teardrop, 10 × 15mm
1 gilt-plated daisy-wheel bead, 8mm
2 gilt-plated corrugated metal beads, 4mm
2 gilt-plated metal beads, 3mm

2 gilt-plated 'leaf' bead caps, 10mm
1 gilt-plated hatpin, 13cm (5in)
1 gilt-plated hatpin protector
1 gilt-plated small round crimp
Flat-nosed pliers

1 Collect together all your beads and findings and place them in separate shallow containers on a tray.

2 To make up the hat- or lapel pin, follow the photograph below and the instructions for the Cloisonné Hat- or Lapel Pin on page 45.

CARING FOR YOUR PEARLS

Pearls, both real and imitation, are delicate and need gentle handling and special care. The best way to keep them bright is to wear them, but do not put them on before applying hairspray or perfume as the chemicals in such products will destroy the pearly sheen. It is also sensible to keep pearls in a separate compartment of your jewellery box, as other jewellery which is harder may damage them.

THE VERSATILE ROCAILLE

ocaille beads are easily recognisable as the tiny beads used for 'love bead' necklaces. They are made in many countries in a wide range of colours and finishes. I find them essential to all bead jewellery making and there are few projects in this book that do not use them. They are also useful in their own right and, together with their close relations, bugle beads, can be the main component for many lovely necklaces and earrings. Rocaille beads can be threaded and woven, threaded and plaited or formed into colourful daisy chains, like the necklace that inspired me to start jewellery making.

When you begin to make jewellery with rocaille beads you will soon want to experiment and produce your own styles. Here I have had to limit the projects to just a few of the possibilities, although the accompanying photographs show some other designs which I hope will encourage you to try creating your own.

· Daisy Chain ·

This pretty necklace makes an unusual gift for a little girl, especially if combined with alphabet beads which spell her name. Once you have mastered the technique for making this simple single daisy chain, the Name Necklace is easily strung using the same skills, following the sequence shown in the photograph on page 55.

Finished length: 53cm (21in)

---

1 packet each small rocaille beads in red, mauve, blue, turquoise and green
1 packet medium black rocaille beads
1 packet small gold-coloured rocaille beads

1 packet black bugle beads, 8mm
1 gilt-plated barrel (screw) clasp
1 length 0.04mm woven-polyester beading thread, 1m (40in)

---

1 Collect together all your beads and findings and place them in separate shallow containers on a tray.
2 Following the instructions for Basic Necklace Threading on pages 19–20, prepare the thread with liquid superglue and tie one end of it straight on to the clasp, following Figs 1a–d for Theresa's Necklace on page 24.
3 Thread on one green rocaille, one black rocaille, one bugle, one black rocaille and one green rocaille.
4 Thread on eight small red rocailles.

5 Pass the threading end through the first of the red beads, forming a loop (Fig 1a).

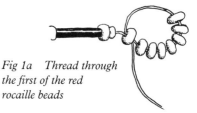

Fig 1a   Thread through the first of the red rocaille beads

6 Gently pull the thread so that the loop sits tight to the other beads.

7 Thread on one gold rocaille (Fig 1b).

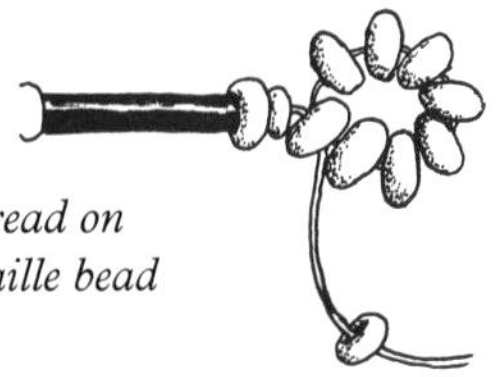

*Fig 1b   Thread on
one gold rocaille bead*

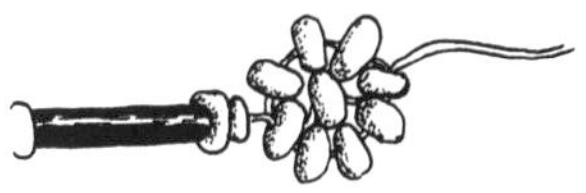

*Fig 1c   Thread through the fourth red rocaille bead to
form the 'daisy'*

8 Pass the threading end through the fourth red rocaille and gently pull it tight so that this bead becomes the eye of the daisy in the centre of the loop of red beads (Fig 1c).

9 To complete threading, continue following steps 3–8 following the colour sequence in the photograph.

10 As step 2, tie the thread to the other end of the clasp.

· Plaited Evening Necklace ·

*This sophisticated necklace is inexpensive to produce and, although time-consuming, is not difficult
to make. It demonstrates the versatility of the simple rocaille. Here I have used a few other small
beads to provide added interest, but you could make a necklace of similar style using only rocailles.
As rocaille beads are available in a huge range of colours, this style, which can include many of
them, is useful when you are trying to make a piece of jewellery to match an outfit. The beads I
have chosen here make a necklace ideal for evening wear.*

Finished length: 56cm (22in)

1 packet each black rocaille beads, small and large
1 packet large dark green, silver-lined rocaille beads
1 packet medium dark blue, silver-lined rocaille beads
1 packet medium black AB coated rocaille beads
1 packet small gold-coloured rocaille beads
21 glass pearls, 4mm
6 each black 'oily' faceted-glass beads, 8mm and 4mm

11 black glass beads, 4mm
14 black glass lozenge filler beads, 6 × 8mm
14 black glass barrel filler beads, 4 × 8mm
11 gilt-plated metal melon beads, 3 × 6mm
2 gilt-plated necklace end caps
1 gilt-plated fob-type clasp
2 gilt-plated headpins, 5cm (2in)
3 lengths woven-polyester beading thread, each 91cm (36in)
Cutting, flat-nosed and round-nosed pliers *or* household pliers

1 Collect together all your beads and findings and place them in separate shallow containers on a tray.

2 Take the three lengths of thread and tie them together at one end using an overhand knot.

3 Following the instructions in Basic Necklace Threading on pages 19–20 dab the knot with gel superglue and prepare the threading ends with liquid superglue.

4 On to each of the three threads, thread on 69cm (27in) of beads in a semi-haphazard sequence. Use roughly equal spacing for the non-rocaille beads; use the small gold-coloured rocailles on either side of some of the special beads to emphasise them; and keep the colours fairly even throughout.

5 When each length is completed tie on a single rocaille, using a loose knot, leaving the threaded beads a little movement on the thread. Do not cut off the spare thread.

6 Plait the whole length of the three threads together. You may need to try this several times before you get the ends to finish evenly.

7 Now comes the tricky bit! You may need an extra pair of hands to hold your plaited beads while you remove the last, loosely tied rocaille bead from each of the threads.

8 Holding the three threads carefully to stop the plaiting from coming undone, tie the threads together using an overhand knot.

9 Dab the knot with gel superglue and cut off all the loose ends of thread.

10 Cut the end off a headpin and make a loop. Before closing this loop, use it to catch up the knot at one end of your necklace (Fig 2a).

Fig 2a   Use a headpin to 'catch' the knot at the end of the necklace

11 Cover the knot and headpin loop by threading a necklace end cap over the straight end of the headpin (Fig 2b).

Fig 2b   Cover the knot and headpin loop with a necklace end cap

12 Cut the headpin to leave approx 1cm (½in) and make a loop which will be used for attaching the clasp.

13 Repeat steps 10–12 at the other end of your necklace.

14 Attach the clasp to each end of the necklace using the loops made in step 12.

·Twist Rocaille Strand Necklace·

A variation on the Plaited Evening Necklace is to thread it in the same manner but instead of plaiting it, leave the threaded beads loose or twisted. If you wish to wear it twisted you must be sure that the clasp chosen will not allow the twist to come undone; this means barrel clasps, which have a swivel loop, are not suitable. An example of this style of necklace is shown in the photograph above. It is made using four threads and very few beads other than rocailles and bugles.

·Wire 'Woven' Pendant·

This pendant-style necklace uses a technique which can be adapted to many designs. It is made using a simple 'weaving' method, and only a little imagination is required to make many more interesting styles. The photograph on page 60 shows the necklace together with an earring which is made in the same manner. I have not given instructions for this as you need only follow the instructions given here and the design as seen. It is important when choosing your rocaille beads for these pieces that the two colours should be of the same size.

Finished length: 66cm (26in)

1 packet medium black AB coated rocaille beads
1 packet medium silver-coloured rocaille beads
15 silver-plated headpins, 5cm (2in)
1 silver-plated barrel (screw) clasp

1 length silver-plated 0.04mm jewellery wire, 91cm (36in)
Cutting, flat-nosed and round-nosed pliers *or* household pliers

1 Collect together all your beads and findings and place them in separate shallow containers on a tray.
2 Start the pendant by threading three silver-coloured rocaille beads into the centre of the length of wire.
3 Take the two ends of the wire and thread them back through the first and last silver rocaille beads (Fig 3a).

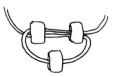

Fig 3a   Thread the wires back through the first and last silver rocaille beads

4 On to one end of the wire thread one silver, one black and one silver rocaille.

5 Thread the other end of the wire back through these beads to form a small triangle (Fig 3b). Pull the wire tight.

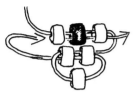

Fig 3b On one end of the wire thread on one silver, one black and one silver bead, and then thread the other end back through these beads to form a small triangle

6 Following Fig 4, continue threading in this way until you have threaded eighteen rows, (including the first rocaille).

7 Finish off by threading both ends of the wire back through several rows (Fig 5).

8 Remove the head from a headpin, make a small loop in one end and pass it through the last line of rocaille beads.

9 Complete the pendant by making a loop at the other end of this headpin.

10 The 'chain' of beads from which the pendant hangs is made by threading the rocaille beads on to headpins, following Fig 4, and then linking the headpins together following the instructions and diagrams for the Enamel Bead Bracelet on pages 29–30.

Fig 4 Diagram of completed pendant to show threading sequence

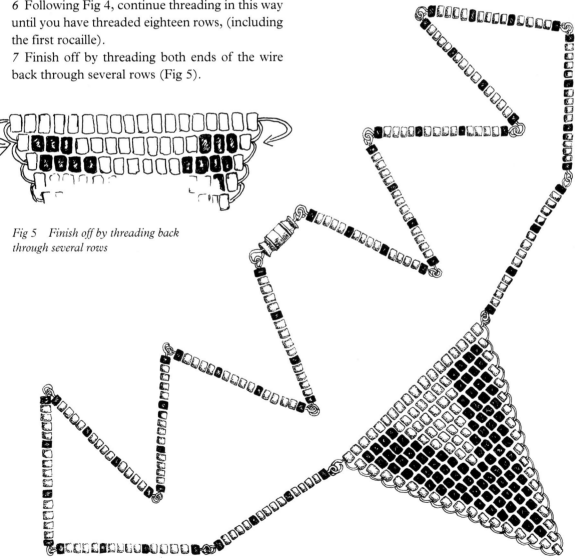

Fig 5 Finish off by threading back through several rows

BOHEMIAN RHAPSODY

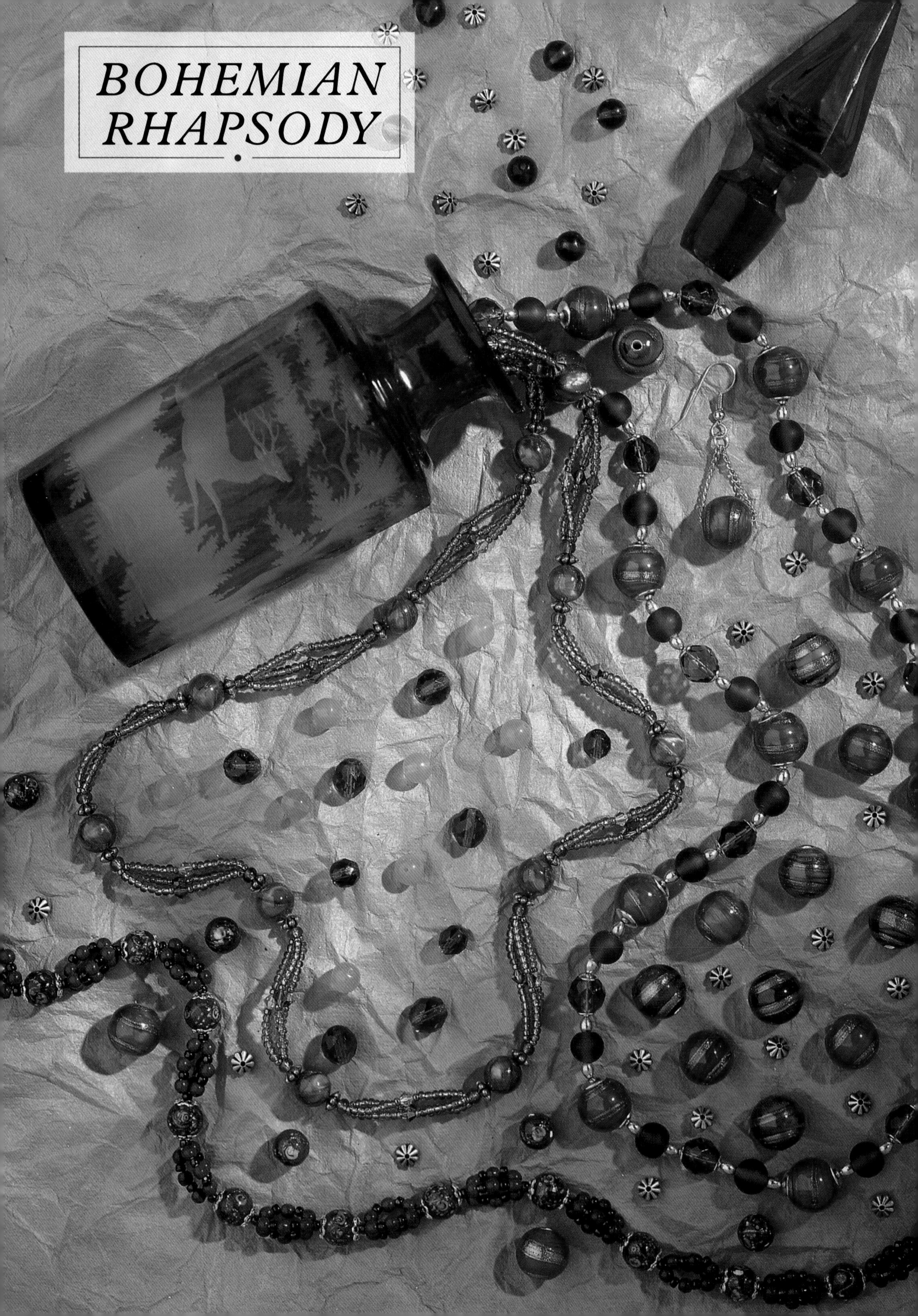

Bohemian glass lamp beads are among the most beautiful and exquisite. Like all lamp beads each one is individually handmade, but these seem to have a special lustre and depth of colour, with a sheen almost like the silkiest satin. Their quality is reflected in the price they command, which is higher than the majority of glass beads. For this reason, when making a necklace with Bohemian beads it is often necessary to limit the quantity used. In doing this, try to show them off to best advantage by a careful choice of other beads which will allow the special ones to retain their significance. The designs which follow show some of these lovely beads in use.

·*A Touch of Glitz*·

This triple-strung necklace is made using just eleven Bohemian glass beads. They are a beautiful mauve in colour, which varies in intensity and incorporates a swirl of dark goldstone under a satiny finish. The beads chosen as companions enhance all these qualities without becoming overpowering. There are tiny silver-lined mauve rocailles, Czechoslovakian crystal, and bronze rocaille that are given their colour by the addition of real gold.

Finished length: 69cm (27in)

11 mauve Bohemian glass beads, 10mm
12 each faceted-glass bicones, 4mm, in dark mauve, light mauve and dark AB coated
22 gilt-plated daisy-wheel beads, 8mm
1 packet small bronze-coloured rocaille beads
1 packet mauve, silver-lined rocaille beads, 5mm
2 packets small mauve, silver-lined rocaille beads
2 gilt-plated calottes
1 gilt-plated fancy box clasp
3 lengths woven-polyester beading thread, each 84cm (33in)

1 Collect together all your beads and findings and place them in separate shallow containers on a tray. As this triple-strung necklace is made chiefly of rocailles and other small beads it is impractical to use a beading tray for order of threading.

2 Following steps 2 and 3 for the Victorian Black Tassel necklace on page 33, join the three threads together and prepare the ends for threading.

3 Take one of the three prepared threads and thread on beads in the following sequence: one large rocaille, one small bronze rocaille, seven small mauve rocailles, one small bronze rocaille, one dark mauve faceted-glass bicone, one small bronze rocaille, seven small mauve rocailles, one small bronze rocaille, one large mauve rocaille, one gilt-plated daisy-wheel bead, one Bohemian glass bead and one daisy-wheel bead.

4 Continue this sequence until all the Bohemian beads have been used, finishing with the rocaille sequence as shown in the photograph on page 62.

5 Allowing some slack, tie a spare bead loosely

on to this thread.

6 Take a second thread and thread it through the first large rocaille of the previous thread.

7 Thread on eight mauve rocailles, one bronze rocaille, one light mauve faceted-glass bicone, one bronze rocaille and eight mauve rocailles.

8 Thread through the large rocaille, the daisy-wheel bead, the Bohemian bead, another daisy-wheel bead and the next large rocaille on the first thread (Fig 1).

9 Continue threading in this order to the end of the necklace and finish off as in step 5.

10 Using the third thread, follow steps 6–9 but replacing the light mauve faceted-glass bicone in

step 7 with a dark AB coated faceted-glass bicone.

11 Lay the necklace on a flat surface and, adjusting as necessary by gentle easing and pulling of the threads, make sure that the three threads are of even tension.

12 Keeping the necklace as flat as possible, remove the spare beads from the thread ends and tie the three threads together using an overhand knot.

13 Following the instructions in Basic Necklace Threading on pages 19–20, apply a little gel superglue to the knot, cover it with a calotte and attach the clasp.

Fig 1   Threading the second thread

· Blackberry and Wine ·

The gorgeous rich colours of ripe fruit and red wine are combined here to make a simple necklace of great style. The large beads are Bohemian glass in a very dark, soft, deep pink with a surface swirl of goldstone. Accompanying them, the different textures of Czechoslovakian faceted glass and frosted Indian glass provide a perfect foil. The finishing touch is given by the gilt-plated linking bead and the plain bead caps, which enhance the feature beads.

Finished length: 71cm (28in)

11 dark pink Bohemian beads, 15mm

12 dark mauve Czechoslovakian faceted-glass beads, 10mm

24 very deep mauve Indian frosted-glass beads, 9mm

48 gilt-plated melon beads, 3 × 5mm

22 gilt-plated plain bead caps, 7mm

24 gilt-plated plain bead caps, 5mm

2 gilt-plated calottes

1 gilt-plated fancy box clasp

1 length woven-polyester beading thread, 86cm (34in)

1 Collect together all your beads and findings and, following the photograph on page 62, place the large beads in your beading tray in order of threading. Place the small beads and findings in separate shallow containers on a tray.

2 To make up the necklace, follow the design from the photograph and the instructions in Basic Necklace Threading on pages 19–20, noting that the 7mm bead caps should sit to either side of the large Bohemian beads and the 5mm bead caps should sit to either side of the faceted-glass beads.

· *Midnight-Blue Cufflinks* ·

These cufflinks would make a most unusual gift for the more adventurous man who is happy to stray from traditional style. The beads used are a lovely shade of deep blue with raised goldstone scrolls. This is a simple project which can easily be tackled by anyone who has learned the Basic Earring Making skills on page 21.

4 blue Bohemian beads, 10mm	2 lengths fine 'gold' chain, each 16cm (¾in)
4 gilt-plated plain bead caps, 7mm	Cutting, flat-nosed and round-nosed pliers *or*
4 gilt-plated headpins, 5cm (2in)	household pliers

1 Collect together all your beads and findings and place them in separate shallow containers on a tray.

2 Thread a 7mm bead cap and then a 10mm bead on to the first headpin

3 Cut the spare wire from the headpin, leaving enough to make a loop.

4 Form a loop in the remaining headpin wire. Before closing it, thread the wire through the last link at one end of the chain. Close the loop.

5 Repeat steps 2–4 using another 10mm bead, 7mm bead cap and headpin at the other end of the chain.

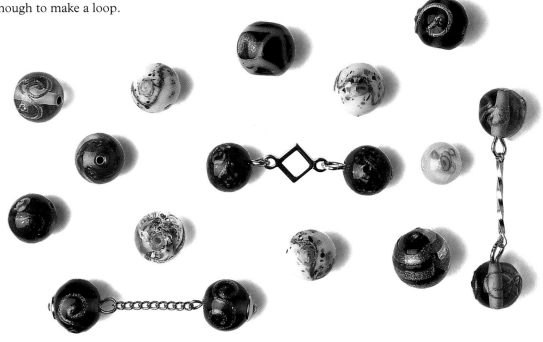

JEWELS FROM THE EARTH

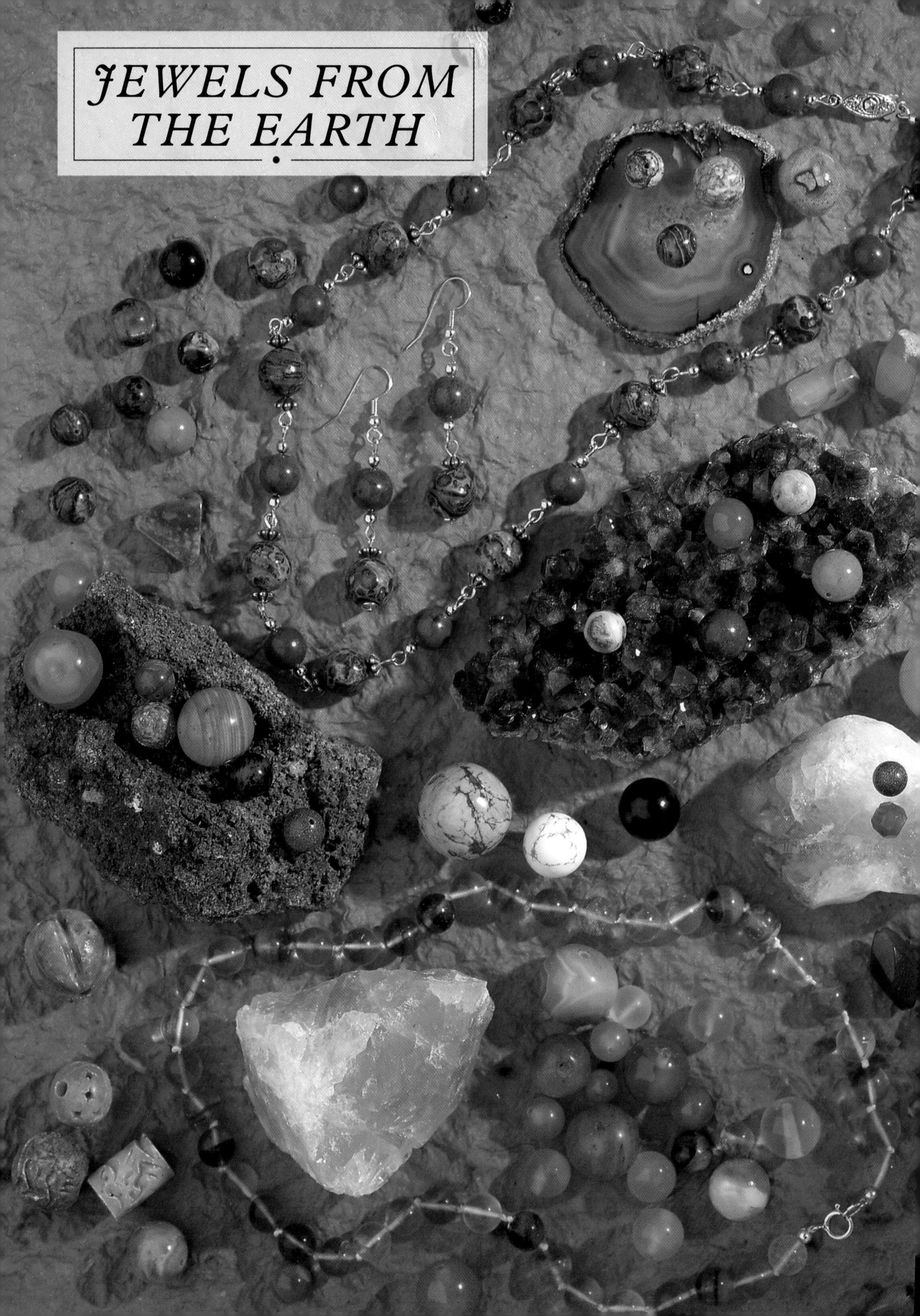

A surprising number of today's beads are made from semi-precious stone. For thousands of years, from the much-prized lapis lazuli of ancient Egypt to the dyed fossil stone of our era, stone hewn from the earth has been turned into beads and used by man for adornment and trade.

Today we are fortunate in having a very wide choice of semi-precious beads available at reasonable prices. Many are, in fact, cheaper than beads manufactured from man-made materials. The colour range is vast: there is garnet (deep glowing red), lapis lazuli (rich royal blue), tiger eye (golden-brown), malachite (banded deep soft green) and amethyst (pale to dark mauve), to mention just the few that everyone will know. The list could go on for pages just to cover naturally occurring stone colours, but then there are also the dyed stones. Some of these are simply poorer quality semi-precious stones which have been colour enhanced to give a better appearance – this applies particularly to turquoise and lapis lazuli. Others, such as dyed fossil stone (limestone), do not pretend to be semi-precious and sometimes appear in vibrant colours such as pink, red or purple. An attractive bead that is often dyed to the colour of lapis lazuli or turquoise is howlite. In its natural form this stone is pure white with grey marbling and beads made from it are available in large sizes at very little cost.

A frustrating fact about many semi-precious stone beads is that the holes are often very small. This is because they are sold by weight, and obviously the smaller the hole the greater the weight and therefore the profit! Not only are the holes small but they are often made by drilling from either end, and sometimes the two drilled holes do not meet exactly. In practice these two problems can mean that out of a loose-strung length of beads (this is the way they are normally sold) a few will be quite unusable except on the monofilament nylon on which they were probably originally strung. Depending on the hardness of the stone, you may be able to enlarge the hole by forcing a headpin through it.

In many jewellery shops semi-precious stone beads are used in a most unimaginative way. In this chapter, however, you will find some fresh, new ideas, as well as the traditional method of threading by knotting between each bead.

· Shades of Autumn ·

The colours of autumn leaves inspired the choice of stone for this necklace, which is made from a combination of leopardskin rhyolite and obsidian mahogany. Leopardskin rhyolite are the larger beads with the mottled appearance, which obviously gives rise to the name. They are very useful beads which blend nicely with all shades of grey, brown and black, and they also mix well with other types of bead such as faceted or plain glass. Here, their brown aspect is emphasised by the companion beads, obsidian mahogany. This name suggests beads made of wood but in fact they are a natural stone of volcanic origin, the colour of which varies from black through to rich brown with some beads exhibiting a mix of both colours. For this necklace, black beads were excluded.

Because both these beads are relatively inexpensive and the method used for 'threading' requires very few, the necklace will be quite cheap to produce. It will, however, be rich in appearance and style, and more than worth the extra time taken to make it. The matching earrings complete the classy look, and are made using the same method as for the necklace.

Finished length: 51cm (20in)

10 leopardskin rhyolite beads, 12mm
11 obsidian mahogany beads, 10mm
20 gilt-plated daisy-wheel beads, 8mm
22 gilt-plated metal beads, 3mm

21 gilt-plated headpins, 5cm (2in)
1 gilt-plated fancy box clasp
Cutting, flat-nosed and round-nosed pliers *or*
    household pliers

1 Collect together all your beads and findings and, following the photograph on page 66, place the large beads in your beading tray in order of threading. Place the small beads and findings in separate shallow containers on a tray.

2 To make up the necklace, follow the design from the photograph and the technique described and illustrated for the Enamel Bead Bracelet on pages 29–30.

· *Shades of Autumn Earrings* ·

These simple earrings are made using two headpins per earring to ensure that the style matches the necklace. The joint of the loops also gives more movement, pleasing in longer drops such as this.

2 leopardskin rhyolite beads, 12mm
2 obsidian mahogany beads, 10mm
4 gilt-plated metal beads, 3mm
2 gilt-plated daisy-wheel beads, 8mm

2 gilt-plated plain bead caps, 4mm
4 gilt-plated headpins, 5cm (2in)
2 gilt-plated earhooks

1 Collect together all your beads and findings and place in separate shallow containers on a tray.
2 To make up these earrings, follow the design

from the photograph on page 66 and the technique described and illustrated for the Enamel Bead Bracelet on pages 29–30.

· *Knotted Rainbow-Fluorite Necklace* ·

This method of threading is used most often for valuable beads or those which are likely to be damaged by contact with others. The beads in this necklace are made from a beautiful but soft stone, so knotting between each one provides some protection against chipping. Rainbow fluorite is an inexpensive stone which appears in a range of banded colours that vary from a clear, pale sea green to the deepest 'amethyst'. Sometimes several distinctly different colours appear in the same bead, and in a whole string you will never find two the same.

If you make your knotted necklace from rainbow fluorite do be very careful when handling the beads as they will be harmed by careless knocks against other, harder materials. The thread chosen for this project is woven-polyester beading thread; however, you may wish to use silk, which is the traditional thread for semi-precious knotted necklaces. To produce a large knot the thread is used double, and therefore a beading needle is necessary for threading.

Finished length: 46cm (18in)

KNOTTING BEADS WITH SMALL HOLES

As already mentioned, some semi-precious stone beads have small holes that will not allow the passage of a beading needle and two threads. In this instance, prepare the thread for threading following the instructions in Basic Necklace Threading on pages 19–20 and, when knotting your necklace, if the knot appears too small tie a second one on top of the first.

41 rainbow-fluorite beads, 10mm
2 sterling-silver calottes
1 sterling-silver bolt-ring clasp
1 silver lock ring

1 length woven-polyester beading thread, 2m (79in) (halve this length if threading with single thread)
Beading needle (preferably flexible wire type)

1 Collect together all your beads and findings and place them in separate shallow containers on a tray.
2 Thread the beading needle and with the thread pulled even lengths, tie the ends together using an overhand knot.
3 Apply gel superglue to the knot, cut off any spare thread and cover the knot with a calotte.
4 Tie a simple overhand knot and tighten it as close to the calotte as possible. This is made easier by using a small pointed object, such as a cocktail stick or pointed headpin, which is put through the centre of the loose knot to help hold it in position while tightening (Fig 1).

5 Thread on the first bead and then tie another knot as in step 4.
6 Continue threading on all the beads in this manner, with a knot between each one. Finish the necklace with a calotte as in step 3.

Fig 1   Use a pointed headpin or cocktail stick to help tighten the knot against the bead

·*Jewel-Drop Bracelet*·

This unusual bracelet is both easy and inexpensive to make. The beads used are an assortment of twelve different semi-precious stones, which are threaded on to individual headpins together with a matching faceted-crystal bicone and a metal bead. I have not listed the individual beads that I have used as you will probably wish to choose your own.

12 assorted semi-precious stone beads, 8mm
12 assorted faceted-crystal bicones, 4mm
12 gilt-plated metal beads, 2mm
12 gilt-plated headpins
1 gilt-plated jump ring

1 gilt-plated trigger clasp
1 length gilt-plated curb chain (to fit your wrist)
Cutting, flat-nosed or round-nosed pliers *or* household pliers

1 Collect together all your beads and findings and
place in separate shallow containers on a tray.

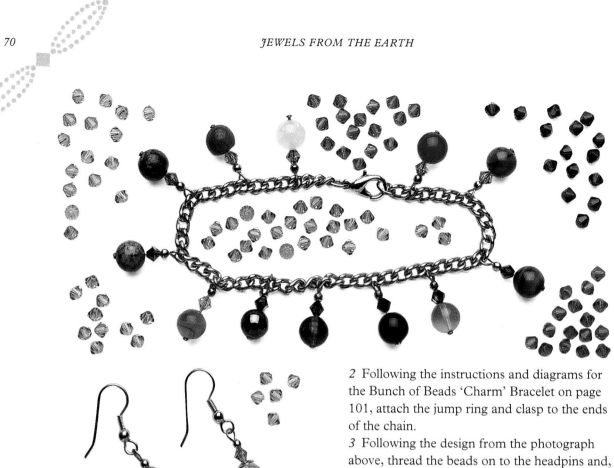

2 Following the instructions and diagrams for the Bunch of Beads 'Charm' Bracelet on page 101, attach the jump ring and clasp to the ends of the chain.

3 Following the design from the photograph above, thread the beads on to the headpins and, following the instructions in Basic Earring Making on page 21, make a loop in each headpin.

4 To complete the bracelet, attach the beaded headpins to the chain at regular intervals.

·Carved Rock-Crystal Earrings·

These delicate earrings are ideal for summer wear. The main beads are made from very clear rock crystal which has been roughly carved and then tumbled to give a soft, rounded finish. The coloured faceted crystals chosen to go with them are only made from glass but have a beautiful, bright sparkle which has a real look of quality.

2 carved rock-crystal beads, 8mm
1 each faceted-crystal bicones, 4mm, in pale blue, pale pink, pale mauve and pale green
4 gilt-plated metal beads, 2mm
4 gilt-plated plain bead caps, 4mm
2 gilt-plated headpins, 5cm (2in)
2 gilt-plated earhooks

1 Collect together all your beads and findings and place them in separate shallow containers on a tray.

2 To make up the earrings, follow the design from the photograph above and the instructions in Basic Earring Making on page 21.

ORIENTAL CINNABAR AND LAC

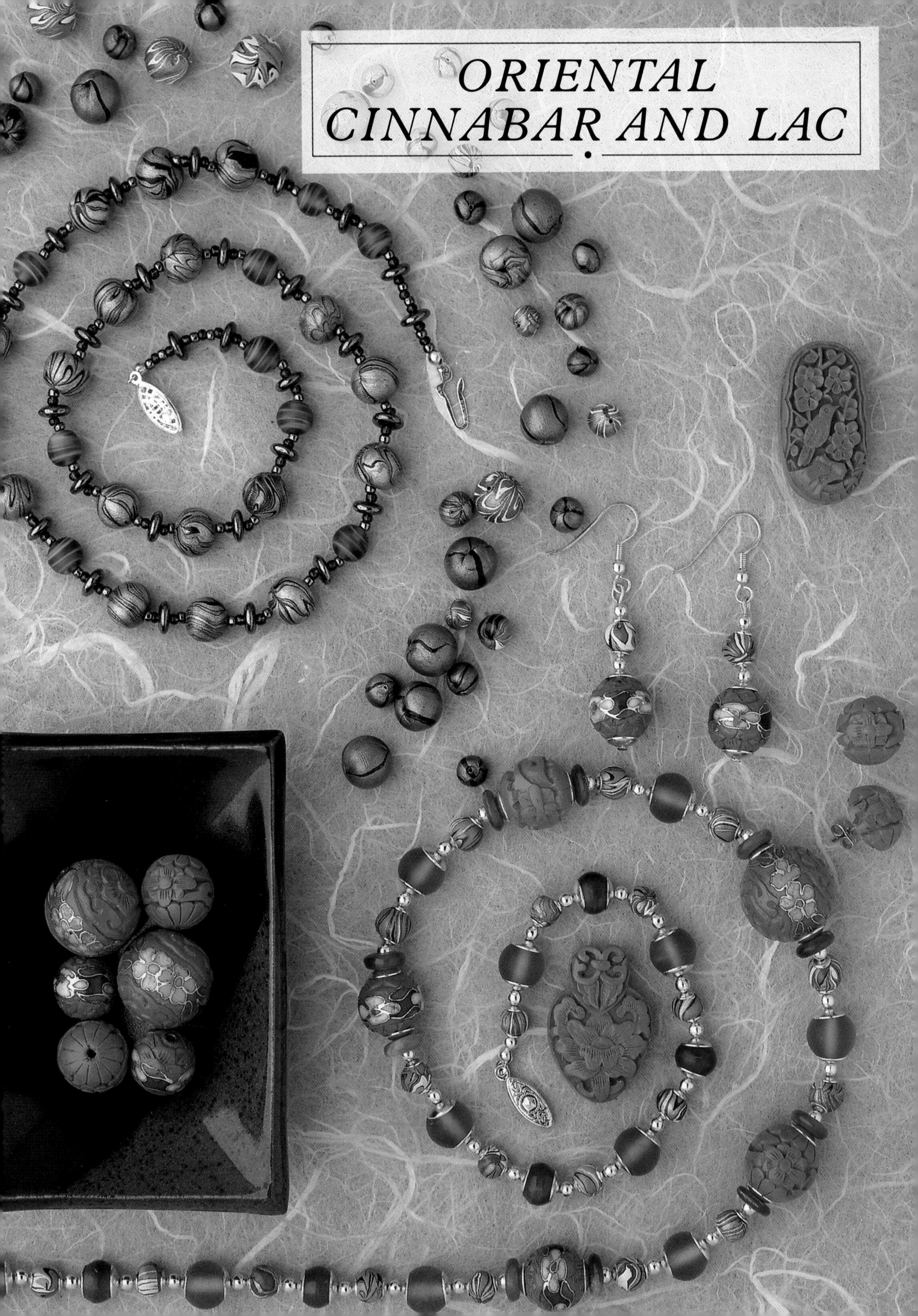

*T*he two bead types used in this chapter are similar in the respect that they are both moulded beads.

Lac beads are made from a resinous substance derived from trees in which the lac beetle makes its home. These unusual beads are obviously handmade and often bear the fingerprint 'signature' of their maker. The surface colour, applied before the bead is completed, is reminiscent of the marbled effect often found inside the cover of an old book. Several colour variations are available, from a sedate silvery-grey marbled with green to a striking, rainbow-rivalling multi-colour.

The material used to make *cinnabar beads* is derived from a mineral – sulphide of mercury. It is treated and applied to a ready-made wooden or metal bead and, when hardened, is hand carved in fine detail. The resulting bead is a bright terracotta red. Those made on a wood base are covered completely with cinnabar, whereas those on a metal base have a band of cloisonné work (see page 10) applied before the cinnabar, giving an unusual and attractive finish.

· *Cinnabar Sensation* ·

To produce a stunning necklace you do not always have to use large quantities of expensive beads. Here just three cloisonné cinnabar and two plain carved cinnabar are used as the feature beads. Cinnabar is a difficult colour to match and on its own can be overpowering, so it is preferable to mix it with beads of other colours and types: here the beads have been chosen to pick up some of the colours in the cinnabar and the cloisonné work. The small Indian lac beads are particularly suitable, as their colours all appear in the cloisonné band and they provide a good link between the green frosted glass, amber horn and cinnabar. At either end of each bead a small gilt-plated bead cap and a gilt-plated bead serve to separate and emphasise the larger beads.

A point worth noting is that horn beads very often have a large hole, and this means that they will not sit centrally over the thread and will cause the beads to lie crookedly. To prevent this happening, after threading on each horn bead thread on enough rocailles of a suitable size to fill the hole and thus hold the bead straight.

Finished length: 66cm (26in)

1 cloisonné cinnabar bead, 20mm
2 each cloisonné cinnabar beads, 15mm and 2 cinnabar beads 16mm
12 green frosted-glass beads, 10mm
24 multi-coloured lac beads, 6–8mm
6 amber-coloured horn beads, 8mm
10 amber-coloured horn discs, 8mm
40 gilt-plated plain bead caps, 7mm

48 gilt-plated plain bead caps, 4mm
48 gilt-plated metal beads, 3mm
1 packet small rocaille beads
2 gilt-plated calottes
1 gilt-plated fancy box clasp
1 length woven-polyester beading thread, 81cm (32in)

1 Collect together all your beads and findings and, following the photograph on page 71, place the large beads in your beading tray in order of threading. Place the small beads and findings in separate shallow containers on a tray.

2 To make up the necklace, follow the design from the photograph and instructions in Basic Necklace Threading on pages 19–20, using the 4mm bead caps for the lac beads and the larger 7mm bead caps for all the other beads.

·Cinnabar Earstuds·

It is not usually possible to make stud earrings using beads – but with cinnabar on wood you can! The matching earrings shown in the photograph on page 71 are made using just the small cloisonné cinnabar and lac beads, together with the bead caps and 'gold' beads. They are simple to make by just following the instructions in Basic Earring Making on page 21.

1 carved cinnabar bead, 16mm
2 earring studs with flat pads, 8mm
2 earring scrolls

Gel superglue
Fine hacksaw blade
Fine-grained sandpaper

1 Using a fine hacksaw blade, saw the cinnabar bead in half, along the length of the hole.
2 Sand down the cut edges to remove any roughness.
3 To complete the earrings glue each half-bead on to one of the earring-stud pads, as shown in Fig 1.

Fig 1   Glue the half-bead to the earring stud

·Silvery Lac with Haematite·

This delicate-looking necklace combines beads from three categories: glass, semi-precious stone and lac. They blend together in surprising harmony.

Finished length: 54cm (21in)

18 silvery lac beads, 12mm
30 haematite discs, 7mm
9 green Japanese frosted lamp beads, 8mm
1 packet small haematite-coloured rocaille beads
2 silver-plated calottes

1 packet medium dark green, silver-lined
   rocaille beads
1 silver-plated box clasp
1 length woven-polyester beading thread,
   69cm (27in)

1 Collect together all your beads and findings and, following the photograph on page 71, place the large beads in your beading tray in order of threading. Place the small beads and findings in separate shallow containers on a tray.

2 To make up the necklace, follow the design from the photograph and the instructions in Basic Necklace Threading on pages 19–20.

PERFECT PORCELAIN

Porcelain beads from China are some of the most delicately beautiful beads available. They are handpainted in a wide range of colours and styles, which vary from pale gold outlined flowers on a pure white base to dramatic white eagles on a black background. The beads themselves are made with great precision and care, as are the boxes in which they are often dispatched. These boxes, also obviously handmade, contain each bead individually wrapped and sitting in its own small square.

·Snakes and Turtles·

The feature beads of this necklace are of a rather unusual design. The scene portrayed seems to be of a snake with its tail entwined around the neck of a turtle or tortoise. I am sure that this pattern must be derived from some Chinese legend or folk tale. The beads chosen to go with them are semi-precious moss agate, whose mix of green and opaque white are a perfect colour match. A long necklace such as this, which includes large beads, sits better on the neck if the large beads are kept to the front, using just the smaller beads close to the clasp.

Finished length: 66cm (26in)

9 Chinese porcelain beads, 18mm
16 moss-agate beads, 10mm
8 green glass beads, 8mm
34 gilt-plated melon beads, 4 × 6mm
18 gilt-plated daisy-wheel beads, 8mm
50 gilt-plated plain bead caps, 7mm
16 gilt-plated plain bead caps, 4mm
2 gilt-plated calottes
1 gilt-plated barrel (screw) clasp
1 length woven-polyester beading thread, 81cm (32in)

1 Collect together all your beads and findings and, following the photograph on page 74, place the large beads in your beading tray in order of threading. Place the small beads and findings in separate shallow containers on a tray.

2 To make up the necklace, follow the design from the instructions in Basic Necklace Threading on pages 19–20, using the 7mm bead caps for the porcelain and moss-agate beads and the 4mm bead caps for the 8mm glass beads.

·Snakes and Turtles Earrings·

These simple-to-make earrings match the Snakes and Turtles necklace. Instead of the usual earhook, here I have used hybrid stud-type earfittings with a surgical steel post and gilt-plated ball. Used together with the earring backs, which have a sterling-silver pad for the part which touches the ear, they should pose no problem for those with metal allergies.

2 Chinese porcelain beads, 18mm

2 moss-agate beads, 10mm

2 gilt-plated daisy-wheel beads, 8mm

2 gilt-plated melon beads, 4 × 6mm

8 gilt-plated plain bead caps, 7mm

2 gilt-plated headpins, 5cm (2in)

2 hybrid earring studs

2 hybrid earring backs

1 Collect together all your beads and findings and place them in separate shallow containers on a tray.

2 To make up the earrings, follow the design from the photograph on page 74 and the instructions in Basic Earring Making on page 21. The only difference in using these earstuds rather than earhooks is that as they have a closed loop, so the headpin loop must be attached before it is closed (Figs 1a and 1b).

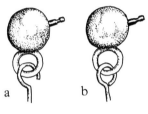

a   b

Figs 1a and 1b Attach the headpin loop to the closed loop of the earring stud

·*Summertime*·

Here is Chinese porcelain in delicately pretty form, with a style of necklace chosen to include tiny glass crystal beads in colours matching those of the handpainted flowers. The necklace is ideal for warm summer days but as all these beads are available in other colours it could be made to suit any occasion. Being triple strung, this project is very similar to All Dressed Up, pages 47–8.

Finished length: 61cm (24in)

13 Chinese porcelain beads, 12mm

168 white-glass beads, 4mm

14 each faceted-glass crystal bicones, 4mm, in pink, yellow and green

26 gilt-plated plain bead caps, 7mm

1 packet small white rocaille beads

2 gilt-plated calottes

1 gilt-plated fancy box clasp

3 lengths 0.04mm woven-polyester beading thread, each 79cm (31in)

1 Collect together all your beads and findings and place them in separate shallow containers on a tray. This is another necklace for which the use of a beading tray is unnecessary.

2 To make up the necklace, follow the threading instructions for All Dressed Up on pages 47–8 and the design as shown in the photograph on page 74 and in Fig 2. This diagram shows three sequences of threading, which should be repeated throughout the necklace to keep the crystal bicones in their correct positions.

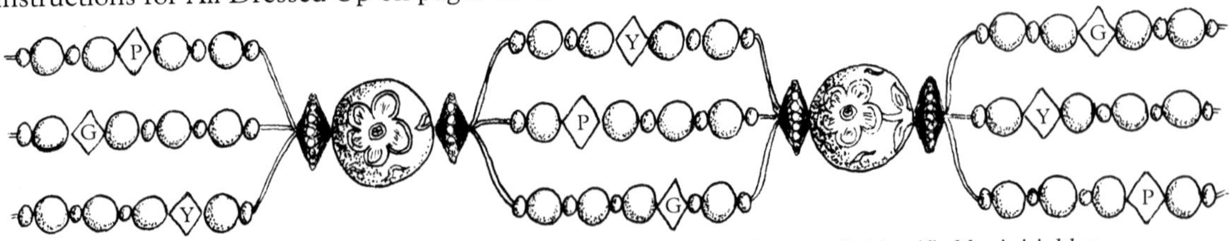

Fig 2   Threading sequence for Summertime necklace, with the colours of the crystals identified by initial letter

Ceramic beads are made all over the world and range from simple clay spheres to finely detailed, handpainted objects of beauty. In this chapter you will find examples which show the diversity of the world's ceramic beads. They come from Crete, Peru, Africa and Thailand.

·*Thailand Terracotta*·

This necklace is made from beads purchased in a Bangkok market and is included to show what can be made from inexpensive beads picked up whilst holidaying in a foreign country. They are obviously handmade, as the fingerprints of their maker can be seen clearly on the surface of many of the beads. The material used is a natural clay which, left unpainted, relies on an impressed pattern for decoration. Originally unimaginatively strung on monofilament nylon, the beads looked dull and unattractive. Here, the use of tiny 2mm gilt-plated and Italian gilt-plated metallised plastic beads as spacers gives the clay beads a lift and helps to produce a beautifully restyled necklace.
It may be difficult for you to find exactly the same beads as those shown here, but you should be able to make a similar necklace following the sizes of bead as listed below. Or you could, of course, make your own copies of the clay beads using a traditional clay, or oven- or air-drying 'clay' – see Do it Yourself, page 122.

Finished length: 51cm (20in)

34 clay beads, 5mm	2 oval clay beads, 12 × 18mm
3 clay beads, 14mm	34 gilt-plated metal beads, 2mm
12 half-round clay beads, 14mm	2 gilt-plated calottes
12 gilt-plated metallised-plastic hogans, 7mm	1 gilt-plated barrel (screw) clasp
6 gilt-plated metallised-plastic flat cushion beads, 10mm	1 length woven-polyester beading thread, 66cm (26in)

1 Collect together all your beads and findings and, following the photograph on page 77, place the large beads in your beading tray in order of threading. Place the small beads and findings in separate shallow containers on a tray.
2 To make up the necklace, follow the design from the photograph and the instructions in Basic Necklace Threading on pages 19–20.

· *Cretan Memories* ·

Visitors to Crete (or any part of Greece) will be familiar with the traditional string of worry beads, and this necklace is made from three strings of Greek ceramic worry beads purchased in a typical gift shop. Various types of beads are used for this purpose but I chose these because they are also available from bead suppliers. The other beads used are Taiwanese miracle and clay beads and 2mm gilt-plated beads. The rocaille beads are not seen in the finished necklace as they are used only to fit inside the large holed ceramic beads and keep them straight on the thread. Designing the necklace was very difficult and it nearly didn't make it to these pages. However, by following this illustration your problems will only be those of threading so many beads and bead caps (786 in total) in correct order! The end result will reward your efforts and, if the beads were bought on holiday, will be a lovely reminder of days in the warm Grecian sun.

Finished length: 66cm (26in)

44 Greek decal beads, 12mm
32 Taiwanese miracle beads, 8mm
74 Taiwanese clay beads, 5mm
158 gilt-plated metal beads, 2mm
2 gilt-plated metal melon beads, 4 × 6mm
212 gilt-plated plain bead caps, 4mm
88 gilt-plated plain bead caps, 7mm

5 gilt-plated shaped triple-spacer bars, 3cm (1⅛ in)
6 gilt-plated calottes
1 packet medium rocaille beads (any colour)
1 gilt-plated fob clasp for triple thread
3 lengths woven-polyester beading thread, each 76cm (30in)

1 Collect together all your beads and findings and place them in separate shallow containers on a tray. There are so many beads in this necklace that it is impractical to use a beading tray though if you wish you could lay out the beads for one length of thread at a time.

2 Following the instructions in Basic Necklace Threading on pages 19–20, prepare the three threads for threading and attach calottes to the other ends.

3 Attach calottes to one end of the clasp (Fig 1).

Fig 1 Attach the three calottes to the clasp loops

4 Following the design from the illustration above, thread the beads and spacers on to all three threads. Do not attach the finishing

calottes, but tie on spare beads loosely until you have checked that the necklace hangs correctly. It may be necessary to adjust the length of one or more threads by the addition or subtraction of some beads. This could be from both ends, in which case you would have to sacrifice one or

more of your original calottes in order to thread on or remove beads. You should only need to make these adjustments if some of your beads are very irregular in size.

5 When you are satisfied that the necklace will hang correctly, attach the calottes and clasp.

·Cretan Memories Earrings·

After making the Cretan Memories necklace, a simple project such as this could be just what you need! The main bead is the same as those used in the necklace, but as an alternative I have chosen a faceted-glass bead as its companion.

2 Greek decal beads, 12mm
2 brown faceted-glass beads, 8mm
4 gilt-plated melon beads, 3 × 5mm

4 each gilt-plated plain bead caps, 7mm and 5mm
2 gilt-plated headpins, 5cm (2in)
2 gilt-plated earhooks

1 Collect together all your beads and findings and place them in separate shallow containers on a tray.

2 To make up the earrings, follow the design from the photograph on page 77 and the instructions in Basic Earring Making on page 21.

· Peruvian Clay·

Many beautiful Peruvian beads come from the Urubamba river-valley region, where the centre of the country's beadmaking is the village of Pisac. Here, beads are made from clay which is processed in the village, formed into beads of all shapes and fired in large earthenware pots. After firing, and when the beads are cool, the handpainted decoration is applied. This is often geometric in style, but also frequently depicts scenes taken from the life of the people and the surrounding countryside.

For this project the beads chosen have a glazed finish, which has been applied after the decoration and before a second firing in the kiln. The partially geometric design incorporates a stylised bird which looks like a pelican – perhaps a resident of the region! The brown beads, which are included for their colour, are dyed fossil stone, the natural colour of which is pale grey.

Finished length: 53cm (21in)

5 Peruvian clay beads, 14mm
28 brown dyed fossil-stone beads, 8mm
18 gilt-plated hogans, 7mm
10 horn discs, 9mm
1 packet small gold-coloured rocaille beads

2 gilt-plated calottes
1 gilt-plated fancy box clasp
1 length woven-polyester beading thread, 69cm (27in)

1 Collect together all your beads and findings and, following the photograph below, place the large beads in your beading tray in order of threading. Place the small beads and findings in separate shallow containers on a tray.

2 To make up the necklace, follow the design from the photograph and the instructions in Basic Necklace Threading on pages 19–20.

· *Peruvian Teardrop Earrings* ·

These earrings are made from unglazed clay beads whose decoration depicts a desert scene with cactus, llama, birds, a man in a sombrero and distant mountains. You would think it impossible to fit so much detail into so small an area! The spiral wires used for these earrings resemble a small, loose spring, coiled tightly at either end. The last loop of the coil at one end is left raised for use as a hanger (Fig 2a). I prefer not to use this loop as it is off centre, causing the spiral to hang crookedly.

2 gilt-plated spiral wires, 12mm
2 Peruvian teardrops
8 gilt-plated metal beads, 3mm
2 gilt-plated headpins, 5cm (2in)
2 earhooks

1 Using the tip of the flat-nosed pliers, flatten the loop of the spiral (Fig 2b).

2 Using your fingers, stretch the spiral wire until it is approximately the same length as the teardrop bead.

3 On to one headpin, thread one 3mm bead.

4 Pass the headpin through the hole at one end of the wire spiral (Fig 2c).

5 Thread on another 3mm bead, the teardrop bead and a third 3mm bead.

6 Stretch the spiral enough to allow the top of the headpin to be threaded through the top hole of the spiral wire (Fig 2d).

7 Thread on the last 3mm bead and cut off any spare wire, leaving enough to make a loop following the instructions in Basic Earring Making on page 21. Attach the earhook.

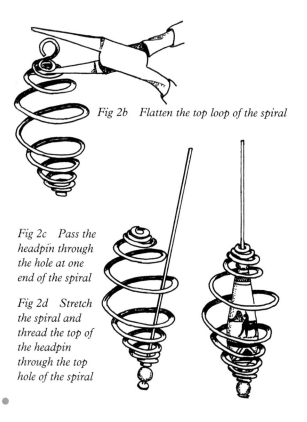

Fig 2b   Flatten the top loop of the spiral

Fig 2c   Pass the headpin through the hole at one end of the spiral

Fig 2d   Stretch the spiral and thread the top of the headpin through the top hole of the spiral

Fig 2a   Spiral wire with hanging loop at the top

·*African Keyring*·

The main bead used for this classy keyring, suitable for a man or woman, is an African clay bead. Beads such as these are made in villages where their manufacture provides valued employment for the local people. They are available in a wide range of colours, from the vibrantly bright to the subdued and natural hues shown here. The keyring used is a very simple and inexpensive type consisting of just a large split ring and chain. An alternative keyring is also shown below.

1 African ceramic bead, 25mm
1 gilt-plated plain bead cap, 7mm
1 gilt-plated hogan, 7mm
1 gilt-plated metal bead, 4 × 6mm
1 gilt-plated headpin, 5cm (2in)
1 gilt-plated keyring with chain
Cutting, flat-nosed and round-nosed pliers *or* household pliers

1 Collect together all your beads and findings and place them in separate shallow containers on a tray.

2 To make up the keyring, follow the design from the photograph and the instructions in Basic Earring Making on page 21.

BEADS FROM NATURE

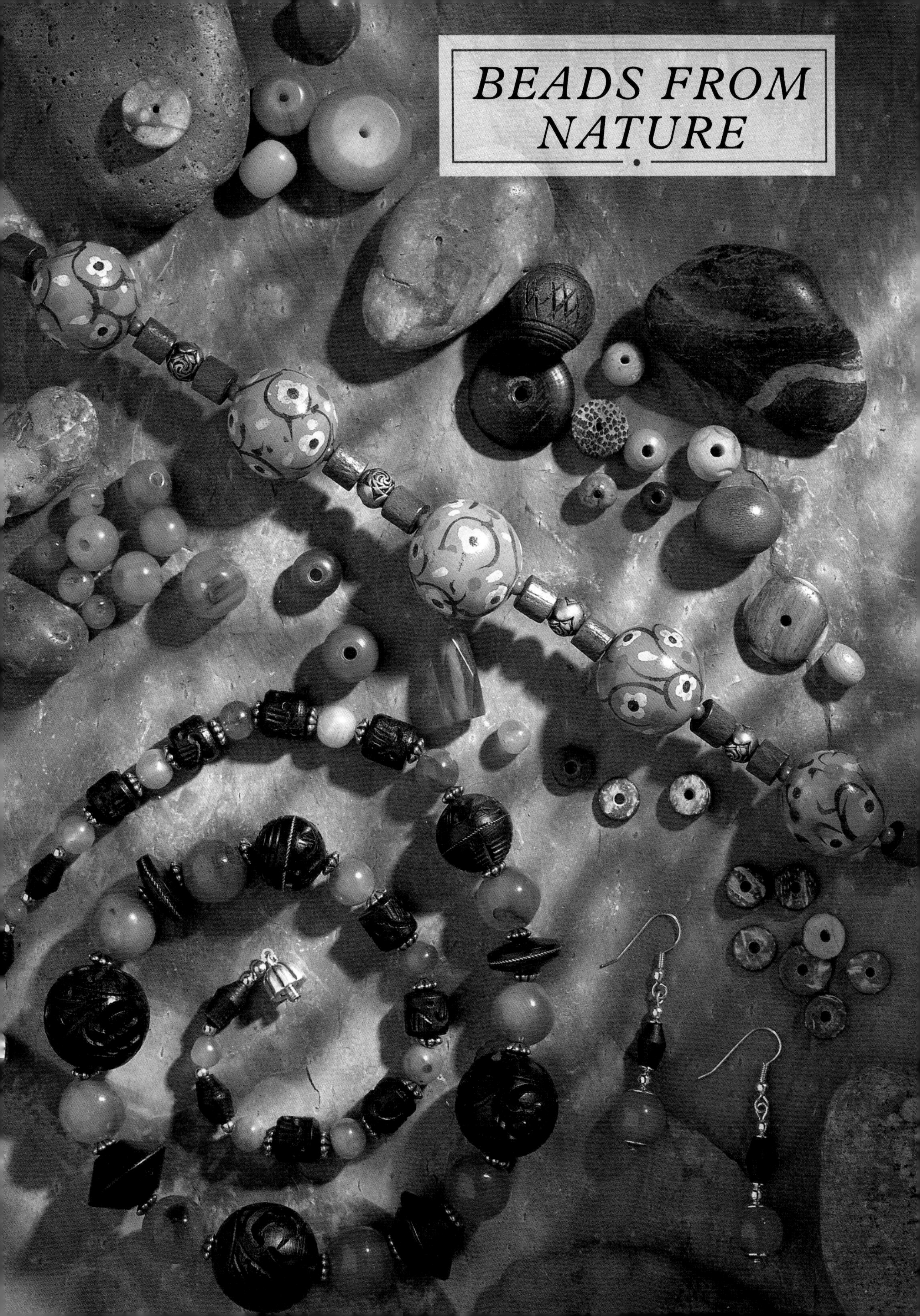

Beads made from natural substances have been used for many thousands of years, and simple drilled seeds, bones and teeth were among our earliest adornments. Today we have become more sophisticated, and beads made from bone, horn, wood and even fruit stones are worked in ways that make them very useful to the modern bead jewellery enthusiast.

The majority of wooden beads come from India and are available in great variety, from the dark and mysterious ebony and warm-coloured rosewood, to huge 35mm handpainted fun beads depicting animals and flowers. The latter are probably more at home as keyring fobs or decorative light pulls than as jewellery, though if you wished you could also use them to make a really chunky necklace.

Another interesting and useful bead from India is the polished horn bead. The horn is treated to make it safe for use and then dyed to various colours from black to amber. Beads made from horn are available in a great many sizes and shapes, usually with a highly polished finish and sometimes with a decorative brass or mother-of-pearl inlay.

Like horn, bone is also treated and dyed – either black, white or cream – and fashioned into many styles of bead. Many are quite elaborately carved into fancy shapes such as birds and animals, which provide unusual earring drops.

· Floral Amber ·

This simple-to-string necklace could be made easily by a child. The main beads used are handpainted wood with a lovely shade of amber as a background to the creamy flowers. Most of the other beads are also wood, with just a few short glass bugles and some gilt-plated rose beads.

Finished length: 56cm (22in)

5 painted wood beads, 25mm
14 wooden barrels, 8 × 8mm
6 wooden melons, 8 × 10mm
4 gilt-plated rose beads, 10mm
34 brown glass beads, 4mm
12 brass beads, 3mm

24 short, large bugle beads, 3 × 3mm
1 gilt-plated barrel (screw) clasp
2 gilt-plated calottes
1 length woven-polyester beading thread, 71cm (28in)

1 Collect together all your beads and findings and, following the photograph on page 83, place the large beads in your beading tray in order of threading. Place the small beads and findings in separate shallow containers on a tray.
2 To make up the necklace, follow the design from the photograph and the instructions in Basic Necklace Threading on pages 19–20. You will see from the photograph that I did not use calottes to attach the clasp, but I would recommend that you do as the finish is much neater.

· Exotic Ebony ·

This simply threaded and designed necklace relies on the contrasting colour and texture of ebony against that of carnelian for its effect. Ebony is a very heavy, dense wood which when polished has a subtle gloss that improves with wear. Six different styles of ebony bead are used here; some of them are hand carved and two have a twisted brass-wire inlay. The Indian carnelian beads which accompany the ebony are often imperfect spheres with holes that are not always central and 'markings' which vary greatly, but this is part of their charm and seen against the darkness of the ebony they appear to glow with their own light. You may not be able to get carnelian beads in the exact sizes stated, but this is unimportant and the beads may not always match their counterparts. In effect, such imperfections only serve to enhance the individual quality of each necklace.

Finished length: 63cm (25in)

3 carved-finish ebony beads, 25mm
2 plain ebony discs, 20mm
2 ebony discs with brass-wire inlay, 15mm
2 carved-finish ebony beads with brass-wire inlay, 15mm
8 carved-finish ebony barrels, 10 × 10mm
4 ebony bicones, 6 × 10mm
8 each carnelian beads, 14mm and 8mm (both approx)

2 each carnelian beads, 10mm and 6mm (both approx)
34 gilt-plated daisy-wheel beads, 8mm
8 gilt-plated metal beads, 3mm
2 gilt-plated calottes
1 gilt-plated metallised-plastic barrel (screw) clasp
1 length woven-polyester beading thread, 79cm (31in)

1 Collect together all your beads and findings and, following the photograph on page 83, place the large beads in your beading tray in order of threading. Place the small beads and findings in separate shallow containers on a tray.
2 To make up the necklace, follow the design from the photograph and the instructions in Basic Necklace Threading on pages 19–20.

· Ebony and Carnelian Earrings ·

These earrings match the Exotic Ebony necklace and are very simple to make.

2 carnelian beads, 12mm
2 ebony bicones, 6 × 10mm
4 gilt-plated metal beads, 3mm
2 each gilt-plated plain bead caps, 7mm and 4mm

2 bugle beads, 10mm
2 gilt-plated headpins, 5cm (2in)
2 gilt-plated earhooks

1 Collect together all your beads and findings and place them in separate shallow containers on a tray.
2 To make up the earrings, follow the design from the photograph on page 83 and the instructions in Basic Earring Making on page 21.

·Squares and Circles·

Here a combination of many different types of bead produces a most unusual and attractive necklace. The flat, square beads and discs are made from polished horn and the black circles from dyed bone. Other beads used are Indian glass, Czechoslovakian glass 'jet', gilt-plated hogans, 3mm 'gold' metal beads and a few tiny black rocaille beads. The only difficulty you may experience in making this necklace is in fitting the glass beads inside the bone circles. To get a good fit, here some very tiny black rocailles have been threaded on either side of the glass bead. As the large beads are handmade and vary in size, it may be that yours are slightly larger or smaller. If this is the case, you will need to make adjustments by either leaving out the small black rocailles or by using larger ones.

Finished length: 71cm (28in)

4 flat, square polished horn beads, 20mm
20 polished horn discs, 10mm
5 black carved-bone circles, 25mm
11 amber-coloured oval glass beads, 10 × 15mm
20 'jet' faceted-glass teardrops, 5 × 10mm
20 gilt-plated hogans, 6mm

16 gilt-plated metal beads, 3mm
10 tiny black rocaille beads
2 gilt-plated calottes
1 gilt-plated jump ring
1 gilt-plated trigger clasp
Length woven-polyester beading thread, 87cm (34in)

1 Collect together all your beads and findings and, following the photograph below, place the large beads in your beading tray in order of threading. Place the small beads and findings in separate shallow containers on a tray.

2 To make up the necklace, follow the design from the photograph and the instructions in Basic Necklace Threading on pages 19–20.

·*Squares and Circles Earrings*·

These easy-to-make earrings are the perfect match for the Squares and Circles necklace.

2 carved-bone circles, 25mm
2 amber-coloured oval glass beads, 10 × 15mm
2 'jet' faceted-glass teardrops, 5 × 10mm

6 tiny black rocaille beads
2 gilt-plated headpins, 5cm (2in)
2 gilt-plated earhooks

1 Collect together all your beads and findings and place them in separate shallow containers on a tray.

2 To make up the earrings, follow the design from the photograph and the instructions in Basic Earring Making on page 21.

·*Frog and Lion Keyrings*·

Two handpainted wooden beads provide the fobs for these fun keyrings. The lion bead is 35mm round and the frog is 30 × 50mm. The frog bead is too long for a 5cm (2in) headpin, so you should either use a longer headpin or join two together by cutting the head off one, making a loop in each and linking the two together. The join will be hidden by the bead (Fig 1). It should be quite difficult to lose your keys if they are attached to these keyrings!

1 large wooden painted 'fun' bead
2 gilt-plated bead caps, 7mm
2 gilt-plated headpins, 5cm (2in)

1 gilt-plated keyring with chain
Cutting, flat-nosed and round nosed pliers *or* household pliers

1 Collect together all your beads and findings and place them in separate shallow containers on a tray.

2 To make up a keyring, follow the design from the photograph on the right and the instructions in Basic Earring Making on page 21.

Fig 1 Join the two headpins by making loops and linking them together

·*Carved Peach Stones and Horn*·

The colours in this necklace are reminiscent of the rust colours of crisp winter leaves. The two main types of bead used to provide this effect are from very different natural sources: the 'amber' beads are polished Indian horn and the large beads are hand-carved Chinese peach stones. The latter really are exquisite and bear close inspection. They are hand carved in the finest detail, depicting the figures of six people surrounded by what appear to be garlands of leaves. Each person is in a different position – perhaps they tell a story? Even the features of the faces can be detected, although they are only just larger than a pinhead. Understandably, these beads are some of the most costly in the book but, as in other instances, only a few of the expensive beads have been used in this design to keep the price of the finished article to a reasonable level.

Finished length: 66cm (26in)

7 carved peach stones, 16mm
8 polished 'amber' horn beads, 12mm
10 polished 'amber' horn beads, 8mm
24 clear brown glass beads, 8mm
4 clear brown glass beads, 5mm
50 plain 'gold' bead caps, 7mm

1 packet medium-size bronze-coloured rocaille beads
2 gilt-plated calottes
1 fancy gilt-plated box clasp
1 length woven-polyester beading thread, 81cm (32in)

1 Collect together all your beads and findings and, following the photograph below, place the large beads in your beading tray in order of threading. Place the small beads and findings in separate shallow containers on a tray.

2 To make up the necklace, follow the design from the photograph and the instructions in Basic Necklace Threading on pages 19–20.

·Carved Peach-Stone Hatpin·

*This hatpin uses the same carved peach stone as the Carved Peach Stone and Horn necklace,
though here it is combined with a different range of beads, listed below.*

1 fluted 'gold' metal bead, 5mm
1 carved Chinese peach stone, 16mm
1 gilt-plated daisy-wheel bead, 8mm
1 brown Taiwanese miracle bead, 8mm
1 gilt-plated fluted metal teardrop, 5 × 8mm
1 brown glass bead, 4 × 7mm

1 gilt-plated metal bead, 3mm
1 hatpin with protector, 13mm (5in)
1 small gilt-plated crimp
Cutting, flat-nosed and round-nosed pliers
or
Household pliers

1 Collect together all your beads and findings
and place them in separate shallow containers on
a tray.
2 To make this hatpin, simply thread the beads
on to the pin in the order shown in the
photograph on page 88. If the last 3mm gilt-
plated bead is not a tight fit, secure the beads on
the pin by squeezing a small crimp with a pair of
pliers so that it fits tightly over the pin, close to
the 3mm gilt-plated bead.

·Twisted Drop Earrings·

*These earrings are included for those who like large and striking jewellery. The main bead is made
from a lamination of four different types of wood. Several shapes of this type of bead are available,
but this one is my favourite as it is so unusual.
You will notice that each earring uses two headpins with a linked-loop join. This has no effect on
the method of making up; just cut the head off the second headpin before making the loops.*

2 laminated wood beads, 20 × 35mm
6 gilt-plated daisy-wheel beads, 8mm
2 each black glass beads, 6mm and 4mm
2 tan-coloured large rocaille beads
2 gilt-plated metal beads, 3mm
4 gilt-plated headpins, 5cm (2in)
2 gilt-plated earstuds
2 gilt-plated scrolls

1 Collect together all your beads and findings
and place them in separate shallow containers on
a tray.
2 To make up the earrings, follow the design
from the photograph and the instructions in
Basic Earring Making on page 21.

ALL THAT
GLITTERS

Metal beads from countries all over the world are available in a huge range of styles and finishes. They vary from large or fancy beads that will become the main feature of a necklace, to the small, round 2–3mm beads that enhance a design almost without being noticed. The necklaces in this chapter give you some idea of the variety of metal beads available.

· *Egyptian Treasures* ·

Two years ago while on holiday in Egypt I could not resist bead hunting in a bazaar. The reward was several finds, the best of which were some beautiful silver filigree beads, very heavy and of exquisite design. I was assured that they were produced locally, though they do look very similar to silverwork from Turkey. They cost little in money but much in negotiating time, and after surviving numerous cups of 'hospitality' tea to ease the bargaining I emerged with some lovely beads. They were certainly worth the time taken for their purchase and, though bought for selling, they have remained with me as part of the precious memories of that holiday. The necklace was made using just three of these beads and shows what you can do with any such treasures that you may find.

The glass beads are made in India. The large ones have silvery feathering, which makes them perfect companions for the silver filigree beads. All the smaller glass beads are also Indian, and some have a frosted finish which gives a good contrast of texture. The small metal beads again are Indian and they are all silver plated. The finishing touches are provided by the use of bead caps to enhance some of the glass beads, and a handmade silver-plated clasp from China.

Finished length: 77cm (30in)

1 Egyptian silver-filigree bead, 22 × 30mm ⎫
2 Egyptian silver-filigree beads, 25 × 17mm ⎰ You could substitute
8 purple glass teardrops, 25 × 15mm   other similar beads
12 purple Indian frosted-glass beads, 10mm   12 silver-plated Indian metal beads, 3mm
10 purple glass lozenge beads, 10 × 8mm   32 silver-plated bead caps, 4mm
6 purple glass barrel beads, 6 × 4mm   8 silver-plated bead caps, 7mm
1 packet large purple rocaille beads   1 length woven-polyester beading thread,
6 silver-plated Indian metal beads, 10mm   97cm (38in)
4 silver-plated Indian metal beads, 5mm   2 silver-plated calottes
1 Chinese silver-plated clasp

1 Collect together all your beads and findings and, following the photograph on page 90, place the large beads in your beading tray in order of threading. Place the small beads and findings in separate shallow containers on a tray.

2 To make up the necklace, follow the design from the photograph and the instructions in Basic Necklace Threading on pages 19–20.

·*Thailand Silvered Resin*·

The main beads used for this necklace are Indian carnelian, but it is given its character and appeal by the addition of the beautiful Thailand silver. These lovely beads are made by applying resin to a plant stalk, covering it with sheet silver to form the shape and then impressing a pattern on the surface. The bead is then finished by burning away the plant stalk, leaving a hole for threading. For this necklace I have also used some small Indian silver-plated beads and some Indian horn discs.

Finished length: 69cm (27in)

6 Thailand silver beads, 10mm
2 Thailand silver teardrops, 8 × 25mm
2 Thailand silver barrel beads, 4 × 8mm
20 Indian silver-plated round beads, 5mm
18 Indian silver-plated round beads, 3mm
20 carnelian beads, 7mm
4 each carnelian beads, 8 × 12mm and 10 × 20mm

1 carnelian bead, 12 × 20mm
16 Indian horn discs, 9mm
12 large tan-coloured rocaille beads
2 silver-plated calottes
1 silver clasp
1 length woven-polyester beading thread, 86cm (34in)

1 Collect together all your beads and findings and, following the photograph on page 90, place the large beads in your beading tray in order of threading. Place the small beads and findings in separate shallow containers on a tray.

2 To make up the necklace, follow the design from the photograph and the instructions in Basic Necklace Threading on pages 19–20.

· *Golden Pumpkins* ·

As a complete contrast to the earlier projects in this chapter, the 'metal' beads used for this necklace are made using modern techniques and materials. The largest have a plastic base which is given a gold-coloured surface (it may also be 'silver' or 'copper'). This finish has a lovely soft appearance and at first glance it would be easy to believe that these are old beads showing the patina of many years' wear. Of the other beads, the small gilt-plated 'melons' are heavy beads machined from solid metal while the faceted-glass beads, chosen for their soft brown colour, are Czechoslovakian crystal.

Finished length: 69cm (27in)

7 gilt-plated metallised-plastic pumpkin beads, 18mm
14 gilt-plated metallised-plastic cushion beads, 10mm
14 gilt-plated metallised-plastic round beads, 9mm
44 gilt-plated melons, 3 × 6mm

14 gilt-plated metal beads, 3mm
22 brown faceted-glass beads, 6mm
2 gilt-plated calottes
1 gilt-plated fancy box clasp
1 length woven-polyester beading thread, 84cm (33in)

1 Collect together all your beads and findings
and, following the photograph below, place the
large beads in your beading tray in order of
threading. Place the small beads and findings in
separate shallow containers on a tray.

2 To make up the necklace, follow the design
from the photograph and the instructions in
Basic Necklace Threading on pages 19–20. The
positioning of the 3mm gilt-plated round beads
may not be apparent from the photograph – they
should be placed on either side of the large
pumpkins.

· *Golden Cufflinks* ·

*The disc beads used for this project are made from metallised plastic and provide the basis for a
pair of cufflinks that have a distinctive look of quality but are in fact quite inexpensive to produce.
They are made simply, using the loop-making techniques in Basic Earring Making on page 21.*

4 gilt-plated metallised-plastic discs, 14mm	Cutting, flat-nosed and round-nosed pliers
2 gilt-plated headpins, 5cm (2in)	*or*
2 lengths fine curb chain, each 15mm (¾in)	Household pliers

1 Thread a disc bead on to the headpin.

2 Cut the spare wire from the headpin, leaving
enough to make a loop.

3 Form a loop in the remaining headpin wire.
Before closing the loop, thread the wire through
the last link at one end of the chain.

4 Repeat steps 1–3, using another disc bead and
headpin at the other end of the chain.

*T*hreading beads on to leather thong gives a new dimension to bead jewellery making and opens the way to using some of the big, chunky beads in imaginative styles. Necklaces can vary from a single special bead strung in pendant fashion, to elaborate double strings using beads of many types and origins.

The necklace projects in this chapter show you several ways to use leather thong. The leather used for each is plain black and 1mm in diameter. Other colours and thicknesses are available, but the larger thicknesses are probably more suitable for pendants as the holes of many beads are too small to allow the threading of anything wider.

When you have finished making a leather-strung necklace, do take care when handling it as, although the leather is thick and looks strong, it is a natural material which will break if overstretched. It is also possible that it may stretch a little when used with heavy beads.

· *Single-Thong Ceramic and Ebony* ·

This very easy-to-make project uses African ceramic, Indian ebony and solid brass beads to create a necklace of simple but attractive design. Even those with no knowledge of beading techniques could produce this necklace quite quickly.

Finished length: 69cm (27in)

1 African ceramic bead, 28mm
4 African ceramic beads, 18mm
2 Indian ebony beads, 18mm
6 Indian ebony discs, 18mm
2 Indian ebony barrel beads, 10 × 10mm
2 Indian ebony bicones, 6 × 12mm

10 solid brass beads, 8mm
2 brass tubes, 4 × 6mm
2 large gilt-plated calottes, 6mm
1 gilt-plated barrel (screw) clasp
1 length leather thong, 84cm (33in)

1 Following the photograph opposite place your beads in order. After the last ceramic bead shown the sequence is: brass bead, ebony barrel, brass bead, bicone and gilt-plated barrel.
2 Tie an overhand knot at one end of the leather thong, pull it tight and cut off any spare leather close to the knot.
3 Open one of the calottes slightly, fit it over the knot and, making sure the leather protrudes from the hole in the calotte, close it using flat-nosed pliers (Fig 1).
4 Cut the other end of the thread diagonally to

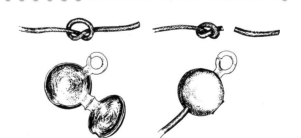

Fig 1   Tie an overhand knot, cut off any spare leather and cover the knot with a calotte

form a 'point' for easy threading (Fig 2).
5 Thread on all the beads in the correct order.

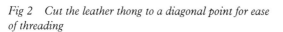

Fig 2   Cut the leather thong to a diagonal point for ease of threading

6 Decide what length you want your necklace and then, allowing an extra 2.5cm (1in), repeat steps 2 and 3.

7 Opening the loops of the calottes, attach the clasp.

8 With the clasp unfastened, hold the necklace up so that the beads slide to a central position. To keep them in this position, tie an overhand knot close to both of the brass tubes.

· *Plaited Thong and Purple Discs* ·

The main beads used in this project are Indian glass discs. Here these simple and inexpensive beads combine with Indian brass to make a most unusual necklace. For a long time these beads were among my stock and I was not able to find a satisfactory use for them until I came up with this design, variations of which have since proved popular. The method for making up this necklace is quite straightforward and requires only simple threading skills and the ability to plait.

Finished length: 57cm (22½in)

23 purple Indian glass discs, 25mm	2 gilt-plated box calotte crimps
8 brass cushion beads, 16mm	1 gilt-plated barrel (screw) clasp
1 length 1mm leather thong, 84cm (33in)	Sticky tape
2 lengths 1mm leather thong, each 61cm (24in)	

1 Collect together all your beads and findings and place them in separate shallow containers on a tray. A beading tray is of no use here as the disc beads will not sit in the groove.

2 Cut one end of the longest leather thong to a diagonal 'point' and tie a loose knot at the other end.

3 Following the illustration (Fig 3) for sequence, thread the beads on to this thong.

4 Undo the first knot and, holding up the two ends of the leather, allow the beads to slide into a central position.

5 To hold the beads in this position, tie a loose overhand knot close to both end beads (Fig 3).

6 Take one of the shorter lengths of leather and thread it through one of the knots you have just tied (Fig 4a).

7 Pull this thong until it is central. You now have three fairly equal lengths of leather which must be plaited to the end (Fig 4b).

8 Use a small piece of sticky tape to hold the

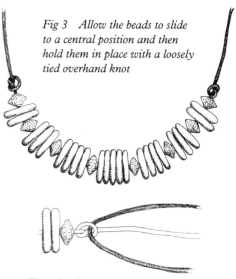

Fig 3   Allow the beads to slide to a central position and then hold them in place with a loosely tied overhand knot

Fig 4a   Thread a shorter length of thong through the knot

three strands together temporarily.

9 Repeat steps 6–8 with the other side of your necklace.

Fig 4b   Plait the three lengths of thong together

10 Measure the two lengths of plaited leather against each other (they never finish at exactly the same length) and, after removing the sticky tape from the shorter one, cut through the three thongs with sharp scissors to make a neat end. Be careful not to let the plaiting come undone.
11 Now fasten the ends of the three thongs together with the box calotte crimp, folding the 'flaps' of the crimp over the leather and squeezing them tight with flat-nosed pliers (Fig 5). Cut off any overlap of thong.
12 Repeat steps 10 and 11 with the other side of

Fig 5   Secure the three plaited thongs together with a box calotte crimp and cut off any overlap of thong

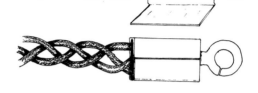

the necklace, making sure that the two lengths of plaiting are equal.
13 Attach the clasp by opening the loops on it and threading on the loops of the calottes. Close the loops using pliers.

·*Variety – A Double-Strung Necklace*·

This necklace combines nearly every type of bead already seen in other projects and shows that you can mix all types, from wood right through to glass, with great effectiveness. The carved Indian ebony and the Chinese cinnabar dominate, with glass, porcelain, brass, metallised-plastic, horn and rocaille beads also incorporated to complement and add extra interest.

Finished length: 76cm (30in)

1 Indian carved ebony bead, 25mm
2 Indian carved ebony beads, 18mm
6 Chinese carved cinnabar beads, 14mm
1 decorated black Indian glass bead, 14mm
2 decorated black Indian glass barrel beads, 10 × 25mm
2 decorated black Indian glass beads, 12mm
2 red Indian glass beads, 10 × 12mm
2 red Indian glass discs, 16mm
4 terracotta-red glass discs, 8mm
4 black crumb-decorated beads, 8mm
2 green and red Chinese porcelain beads, 12mm
2 each brass cushion beads, 14mm and 12mm
4 solid brass beads, 8mm
8 gilt-plated discs, 14mm

4 gilt-plated cushion beads, 10mm
2 gilt-plated daisy-wheel beads, 8mm
4 horn discs, 9mm
2 large dark brown rocaille beads
2 large tan rocaille beads
4 small gold-coloured rocaille beads
2 gilt-plated calottes, 6mm
4 gilt-plated spring crimps
1 gilt-plated hook clasp
6 lengths 1mm leather thong, each 38cm (15in)
1 length 0.06mm woven-polyester beading thread, 41cm (16in)
1 length 0.06mm woven-polyester beading thread, 48cm (19in)
Sticky tape

1 Collect together all your beads and findings and, following the photograph above, place the beads for the shorter string in your beading tray in order of threading. For the moment, place the other beads and findings in separate shallow containers on a tray.

2 Tie two ends of the polyester threads together with a large double knot and, following the instructions in Basic Necklace Threading on pages 19–20, apply a little gel superglue, cut off the spare thread and cover the knot with a calotte.

3 Again following the instructions in Basic Necklace Threading on pages 19–20, prepare the other two ends of the polyester thread for threading.

4 On the shorter length of polyester thread, thread on the beads as laid out in your beading tray. Tie a spare bead loosely on to the end.

5 Following the photograph, place the beads for the longer string in your beading tray in order of threading and then thread them on to the other length of polyester thread.

6 Untie the spare bead from the first thread and, making sure there is no slack in either thread and repeating step 2, tie them together and cover the knot with a calotte.

7 Take three of the lengths of leather and, holding the three ends tightly together, insert them into the non-looped end of one of the spring crimps. The easiest way to do this is to screw the crimp on to the leather (Fig 6a).

Figs 6a and 6b   'Screw' the spring crimp on to the leather thong and, using pliers, squeeze the last coil of the crimp to secure it

8 Tighten the bottom curl of the spring crimp on to the leather by squeezing with pliers. The three ends of leather will now be held securely (Fig 6b).

9 Plait these three lengths of leather together and secure temporarily with a small piece of sticky tape.

10 Repeat steps 7–9 with the other three lengths of leather.

11 Opening the loops of the calottes at the end of the double length of bead strings, attach them to the two loops of the spring crimps.

12 Hold up the nearly finished necklace and decide on the length you want it. Remove the sticky tape and cut through the plaited leather to the required length. Secure the loose ends by following steps 7–8.

13 Using pliers, open the loop of the hook clasp and attach it to the loop of one of the spring crimps.

· *Leather-Thong Earrings* ·

These simply styled earrings are easy and inexpensive to make. The beads used are from India.

2 black decorated glass beads, 12mm	2 silver-plated spring crimps
4 silver-plated metal beads, 9mm	2 silver-plated earhooks
2 lengths 1mm leather thong, each 10cm (4in)	Flat-nosed pliers

1 Collect together all your beads and findings and place them in separate shallow containers on a tray.

2 Thread the beads on to the leather thong following the photograph on the right.

3 Fold the leather thong so that the two ends are together and insert these two ends into the non-looped end of the 'spring' crimp (see Fig 6a for the Variety necklace on page 98).

4 Tighten the bottom curl of the spring crimp on to the leather by squeezing it with pliers (see Fig 6b for the Variety necklace on page 98).

5 Finish off the earrings by using pliers to open the loop of the earhook and attach it to the loop of the 'spring' crimp.

PICK AND MIX

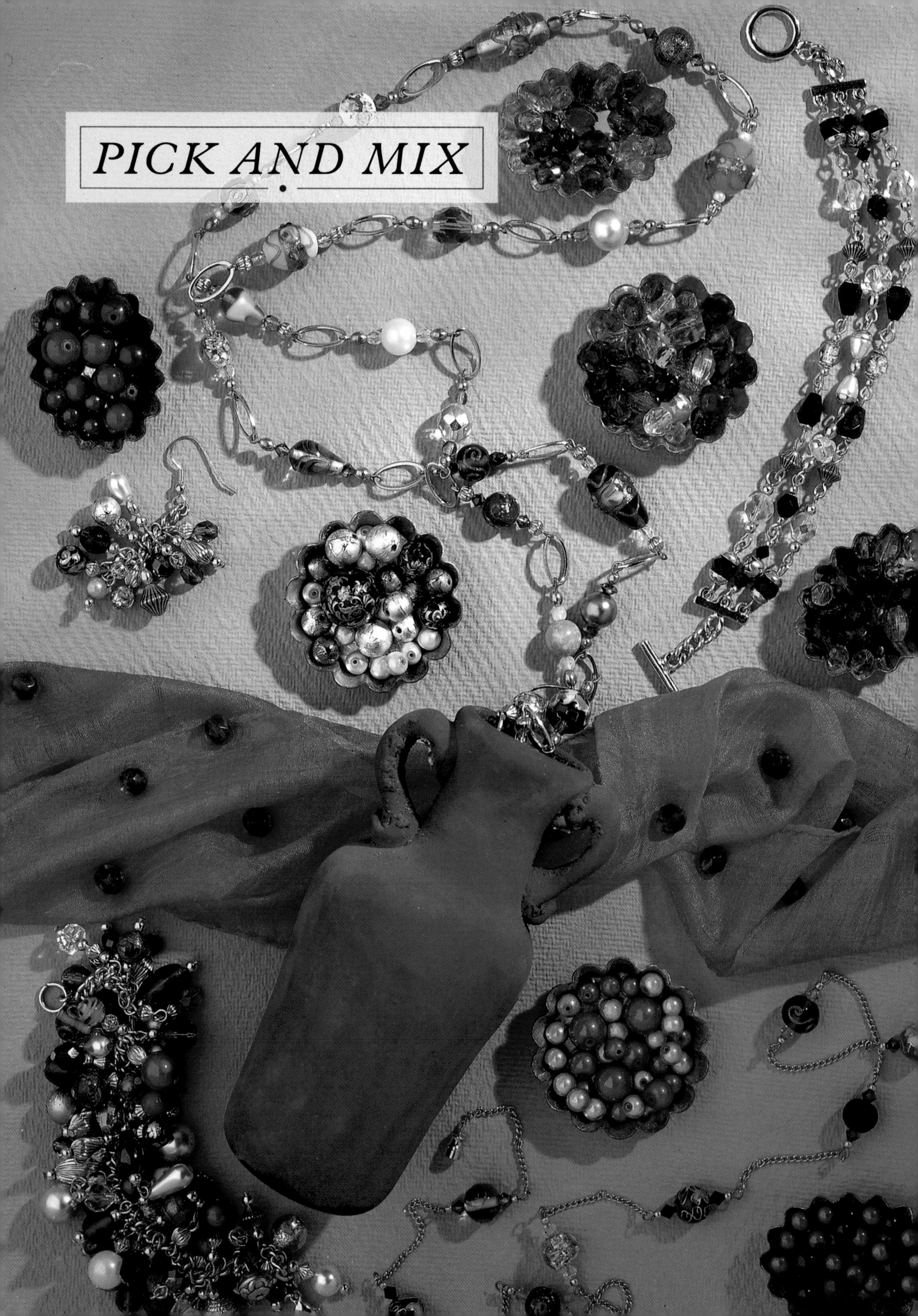

hen you have been making bead jewellery for a while you will begin to accumulate lots of left-over beads. This chapter aims to give you ideas that will make use of these oddments in interesting ways. Collections of unusual beads can also be incorporated into a piece of jewellery.

· Bunch of Beads 'Charm' Bracelet ·

This project is made up using seventy-three different main beads, the largest of which is the 10 × 17mm pearl teardrop and the smallest a 6mm crystal. I have not counted the small metal beads which have been used as fillers, but there are at least a hundred of various types. You could use this design to keep a collection of beads, starting with just one or two and slowly building up the number by adding to them whenever you find a special bead – just like a charm bracelet. This is probably not the best way to look after special beads, but is a lovely way to use them! This bracelet uses many types of bead from at least nine different countries. Some are old beads, some are new. To make the bracelet as here, with lots and lots of beads, is time-consuming but not difficult. The main skill needed is that of making a loop in headpin wire.

1 gilt-plated jump ring, 8mm
Selection of beads of varying sizes, 4–10mm approx (the exact number will depend on your preference)
Gilt-plated metal beads, 3mm ⎫
Gilt-plated metal beads, 4mm ⎬
Gilt-plated headpins 5cm (2in) ⎭

1 gilt-plated trigger clasp
1 length gilt-plated curb chain (to fit your wrist)
Cutting, flat-nosed and round-nosed pliers *or* household pliers

Quantity will vary according to number of large beads used

1 Collect together all your beads and findings and place them in separate shallow containers on a tray.
2 Open the jump ring and attach it to one end of the chain (Fig 1a). Close the jump ring.
3 At the other end of the chain, open the last link and attach the clasp (Fig 1b).
4 Thread a large bead and one or more small metal beads on to a headpin. Following the instructions in Basic Earring Making on page 21, make a loop in the headpin and attach it to a link on the chain.
5 Repeating step 3, continue adding more beads to the chain.

a

b

Fig 1a   Attach the jump ring to one end of the chain

Fig 1b   Open the last link of the other end of the chain and attach the trigger clasp

Fig 2   Attach beaded headpins of varying lengths to the links of the chain

6 To achieve the same effect as the bracelet illustrated, apply at least two beaded headpins to every link, making sure they are of varying lengths with some jointed to give movement (Fig 2). Care should also be taken to balance the colours evenly.

·*Bunch of Beads Earrings*·

These earrings are made by attaching beads to a length of chain in the same manner as for the Bunch of Beads 'Charm' Bracelet. They are fun to make and to wear, though once again a little time-consuming to produce.

1 length of gilt-plated curb chain, 2cm (1in)
Selection of beads of varying sizes, 6–10mm
Gilt-plated metal beads, 3mm }
Gilt-plated metal beads, 4mm }

Gilt-plated headpins, 5cm (2in)
2 gilt-plated earhooks
Quantity will vary according
   to number of large beads used

1 Collect together all your beads and findings and place in separate shallow containers on a tray.
2 Open the loop on an earhook and attach it to one end of the chain.
3 Following steps 3–5 for the Bunches of Beads 'Charm' Bracelet, attach beads all along the length of the chain.
4 If you wish the two earrings to match exactly, make both at the same time, applying bead for bead on each chain.

·*Party-Time Bracelet*·

Thirteen different beads are used in this design and the greatest quantity needed of any one of the large beads is four. The 'ingredients' given below are to make this bracelet as shown, but you could make a similar bracelet using other beads of the same sizes or of random sizes and colours. Although this bracelet looks complicated, it is in fact simple to make and needs only the skills in Basic Earring Making on page 21. Each of the strands of the bracelet are made from beads threaded on to headpins, joined together by linking loops.

4 glass 'jet' beads, 7mm
4 glass 'jet' teardrops, 7 × 10mm
2 glass 'jet' beads, 6mm
4 glass 'jet' bicones, 4mm
4 clear glass crystal beads, 8mm
2 Japanese foiled lamp beads, 6mm
2 carved rock-crystal beads, 8mm
4 gilt-plated hogans, 7mm
2 gilt-plated rose beads, 6mm
2 glass pearl teardrops, 6 × 8mm

5 gilt-plated metal melon beads, 4 × 6mm
8 gilt-plated metal beads, 3mm
12 gilt-plated metal beads, 2.4mm
8 gilt-plated rounded bead caps, 6mm
8 gilt-plated bead caps, 4mm
25 gilt-plated headpins, 5cm (2in)
1 gilt-plated fob clasp for triple stringing
Cutting, flat-nosed and round-nosed pliers
or
Household pliers

1 Collect together all your beads and findings and place them in separate shallow containers on a tray.

2 Following the instructions for Basic Earring Making on page 21, cut the head off one headpin, make a loop and attach it to a loop on the clasp.

3 Following the photograph on page 100 for sequence, thread beads on to this headpin.

4 Cut off spare headpin wire, leaving enough to make a loop. Form the loop.

5 Cut off the head of another headpin, make a loop and attach it to the last loop formed.

6 Thread on the second sequence of beads.

7 Repeat steps 4–6 until the pattern of this 'strand' is complete, attaching the last loop to the other part of the clasp.

8 Repeat steps 2–6 with the other two 'strands' of the bracelet.

9 No matter how careful you are in choosing beads to make three strands of the same length, there are likely to be some slight differences which could spoil the final result. This can be overcome easily by increasing or decreasing the size of some of the linking loops.

·Bead Collector's Necklace·

Like the Bunches of Beads 'Charm' Bracelet on page 101, this style of necklace is a good way to collect and use odd beads. Two different necklaces are photographed but the method for making up is the same. The only difference is that for one I have used jump rings to link the beads and for the other small lengths of curb chain. Other types of link or spacer could be used and more of these can be seen in the photograph of findings on page 15. For a necklace that hangs well it is preferable to use beads of a fairly even size and weight. The instructions given here are for the necklace made using curb chain as the link between the beads. A specific list of beads is not given as the beads you will use will vary from those shown.

Finished length: 66cm (26in)

9 various types of bead, 10mm
18 various colours of faceted-crystal bicones, 4mm
18 gilt-plated metal beads, 2.4mm
9 gilt-plated headpins, 5cm (2in)

10 lengths gilt-plated curb chain, each 4cm (1½in)
1 gilt-plated barrel (screw) clasp
Cutting, flat-nosed and round-nosed pliers *or* household pliers

1 Collect together all your beads and findings and place them in separate shallow containers on a tray.

2 Cut the head off one headpin wire, form a loop and attach it to one end of a length of the chain.

3 Thread your beads on to this headpin, following the photograph on page 100 for order of threading and choosing the faceted-glass bicone beads in colours which complement your 10mm bead.

4 Cut off spare headpin wire and form a loop. Before closing this loop, attach another length of chain.

5 Repeat steps 2–3 until all the pieces of chain are used.

6 Attach the clasp by opening its wire loop, threading on the last link of the chain and then closing the loop.

*F*aceted-glass or crystal beads are available in a multitude of colours, from traditional black glass 'jet' to the most brilliant of hues. All faceted-glass beads are machine cut and many of those available come from Czechoslovakia, though probably the finest and those with the brightest sparkle are made from Austrian Swarovski glass. Faceted beads are very useful in bead jewellery making, especially when the style required is for a dressy evening necklace or earrings. Some faceted glass is made into flat-backed stones and used normally for embroidery. With a little ingenuity this type too can be incorporated into bead jewellery, as you will see in the Amber Teardrop on page 49.

· Smoky Multi-Drop Choker ·

The inspiration for this design came from a Victorian 'jet' mourning necklace, which I have owned and enjoyed wearing for many years – it is photographed with the new designs on page 104. Since acquiring this necklace I have made many 'copies' using a great variety of beads, but the style is so special and dressy that it deserves the glitz of crystal to show it off. This design uses a clear, smoky-quartz colour glass crystal.
Making the necklace involves some skill in threading and in bending headpin wires into loops. It is not difficult, but will provide a little more challenge than simple threading. The length as shown sits just below the neck. You may wish to extend it by adding one or more bead sequences to either side before the drops are threaded on.

Finished length: 42cm (16½in)

15 smoky faceted-glass beads, 8mm round
17 smoky faceted-glass beads, 6mm round
6 smoky faceted-glass beads, 4mm round
57 rainbow-coated faceted-crystal bicones, 4mm
1 packet small haematite-coloured rocaille beads
11 silver-plated plain bead caps, 4mm

23 silver-plated headpins, 5cm (2in)
2 silver-plated metal beads, 3mm
1 length nylon-coated wire, 20cm (8in)
1 silver clasp
Cutting, flat-nosed and round-nosed pliers *or* household pliers

1 Collect together all your beads and findings and place them in separate shallow containers on a tray.
2 Follow the photograph on page 104 and Fig 1 for order of threading, and the instructions for making up given below. The first task is to prepare the eleven drops ready for threading on later.
3 Take two headpins and on each thread: one 4mm bead cap, one 8mm faceted bead, one rocaille, one 4mm bicone bead, and one rocaille. Following the instructions in Basic Earring Making on page 21, cut off spare headpin wire and make a loop.
4 On two more headpins thread on beads as above, followed by one 6mm faceted bead and one rocaille. Make a loop.
5 On two more headpins thread on beads as in

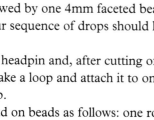

steps 3 and 4, followed by one 4mm bicone bead and one rocaille. Make a loop.

6 On two more headpins thread on all beads as in steps 3–5, followed by one 4mm faceted bead and one rocaille. Make a loop.

7 On two more headpins thread on all beads as in steps 3–6, followed by one 4mm bicone bead and one rocaille. Make a loop.

8 On one headpin thread on all beads as in steps 3–7, followed by one 4mm faceted bead. Make a loop. Your sequence of drops should look like Fig 1.

9 Take a headpin and, after cutting off the 'head', make a loop and attach it to one part of your clasp.

10 Thread on beads as follows: one rocaille, one 4mm bicone bead, one rocaille, one 6mm faceted bead, one rocaille, one 4mm bicone bead and one rocaille. Cut off spare headpin wire and make a loop.

11 Take a second headpin and, repeating step 9, attach it to the spare loop of step 10. Thread on

beads in the previous sequence. Make a loop. Repeat twice more.

12 Repeat steps 9–11 twice more, but replacing the 6mm bead with an 8mm bead.

13 Repeating steps 9–12, make up the other side of the necklace.

14 Using the slip knot described in Theresa's Necklace on page 24, tie the nylon-covered wire to the end loop of one side of your necklace.

15 Following the instructions in Basic Necklace Threading on pages 19–20, cover the knot with a 3mm metal bead. This gives a very neat finish, but as an easier alternative you could attach the wire using a crimp, following the instructions for the Trade-Bead Choker on page 37–8.

16 Lay out the finished drops in order of proposed threading and, following the illustrated design, thread them on to the nylon-coated wire. The sequence is: one rocaille, one 4mm bicone bead, one rocaille, first drop, one rocaille, one 4mm bicone bead, one rocaille, second drop. Continue with this sequence until all the drops are threaded on, finishing as you started with one rocaille, one 4mm bicone bead and one rocaille.

17 Following steps 14 and 15, finish off by tying the nylon-coated wire to the end loop of the other side of the necklace.

Fig 1   Whole necklace to show order of threading

·*Drops of 'Jet'*·

For this elegant evening necklace I have chosen black faceted-glass beads, which are a very good substitute for jet, and teamed them with gold-plated metal 'melon' beads and tiny black rocailles. The techniques used are the same as those for the Smoky Multi-drop Choker, so they are not described in detail again – simply refer to the photograph on page 104 and Fig 1 on page 106. The one slight difference in technique from the Smoky Multi-drop Choker is that to highlight the difference in effect I have used a crimp to join the nylon-covered 'thread' to the end headpin loop.

Finished length: 48cm (19in)

29 black faceted-glass beads, 6mm	1 gilt-plated fancy box clasp
7 black faceted-glass teardrops, 8 × 6mm	1 length of nylon-covered wire, 26cm (10in)
56 gilt-plated melon beads, 3 × 5mm	Cutting, flat-nosed and round-nosed pliers
1 packet small black rocaille beads	*or*
19 gilt-plated headpins, 5cm (2in)	Household pliers

1 Collect together all your beads and findings and place in separate shallow containers on a tray.
2 To make up the necklace, follow the design from the photograph on page 104 and the instructions for the Smoky Multi-drop Choker on pages 105–6.

·*Japanese Decal and Glass 'Jet'*·

These beads have a lovely iridescent peacock- and gold-coloured decoration and are very suitable for a 'glitzy' evening necklace. The secondary beads are 'gold' metallised plastic and some tiny 'gold' rocailles. Here they suit each other very well.

Finished length: 71cm (28in)

3 black Japanese decal beads, 16mm	8 gilt-plated hogans, 6mm
6 each black Japanese decal beads, 12mm and 8mm	22 gilt-plated daisy-wheel beads, 8mm
6 each black glass 'jet' beads, 12mm and 8mm	1 packet small gold-coloured rocaille beads
4 black glass 'jet' beads, 10mm	2 gilt-plated calottes
16 black glass 'jet' beads, 6mm	1 gilt-plated fancy box clasp
2 gilt-plated hogans, 14mm	1 length woven-polyester beading thread,
6 gilt-plated hogans, 8mm	86cm (34in)

1 Collect together all your beads and findings and, following the photograph on page 108, place the large beads in your beading tray in order of threading. Place the small beads and findings in separate shallow containers on a tray.
2 To make up the necklace, follow the design from the photograph and the instructions in Basic Necklace Threading on pages 19–20.

· '*Jet*' *and Decal Earrings* ·

These striking earrings would match the Japanese Decal and Glass 'Jet' necklace, as they are made using the same types of bead. Here a different earring finding is introduced: the 'Go-Go' earfitting. It is a complete change in style from the fittings used so far and is suitable for people with pierced ears. The back, which clips lightly over the post, holds the earring gently in place.

2 black Japanese decal beads, 16mm
2 black glass 'jet' bicones, 10 × 10mm
4 gilt-plated hogans, 5mm
4 gilt-plated fancy bead caps, 10mm

4 gilt-plated plain bead caps, 5mm
2 gilt-plated 'Go-Go' earfittings
2 gilt-plated headpins, 5cm (2in)

1 Collect together all your beads and findings and place in separate shallow containers on a tray.
2 Following the design from the photograph above and the instructions in Basic Earring Making on page 21, thread the beads on to the headpins.
3 When cutting off spare headpin wire, leave a slightly longer length than usual as you will need to make a larger loop for attaching to the 'Go-Go' earfitting.
4 Make a loop and, before closing it, attach it to the lower end of the earfitting (Figs 2a and 2b).

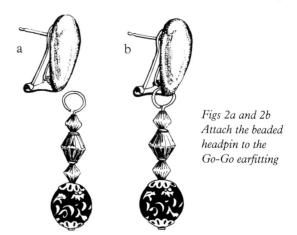

Figs 2a and 2b Attach the beaded headpin to the Go-Go earfitting

*T*his chapter has been included especially for earring fans. Shown here are lots of new styles not seen elsewhere in the book. The earrings are numbered for easy identification and most are very simple to make, following the design from the photograph on page 109 and the instructions in Basic Earring Making on page 21, so for the majority of styles no extra instructions are given. For those that are different, separate instructions are provided. The beads and findings used for each are listed; for details of the pliers required, see Equipment and Materials, page 14.

·*Earhoop with Hanging Bead*·

This versatile pair of earrings can be worn with or without the bead, which can be removed easily by sliding the headpin loop off at the earpost end of the hoop. It is, of course, also a very simple matter to change to a different pair of beads.

1 pair gilt-plated earhoops, 30mm
1 pair clutch backs for earhoops
2 gold-coloured metallised plastic beads, 8mm
2 gilt-plated melon beads, 3 × 5mm
2 gilt-plated plain bead caps, 4mm
2 gilt-plated headpins, 5cm (2in)

·*Gold Flower Trumpet*·

The gold-coloured trumpet finding is the main feature of this pair of earrings. It is through drilled at the top to allow for the threading of a headpin. This trumpet shape is made from plastic and is available in many other finishes from silver to red. The addition of bright 4mm crystal beads hanging like stamens from a central, looped headpin enhances the flower-like appearance.

2 gold-coloured flower-trumpet findings
2 gilt-plated melon beads, 3 × 5mm
2 each faceted-crystal bicones, 4mm, in green, pink, mauve and purple
10 gilt-plated heishi (see Glossary)
8 gilt-plated headpins, 5cm (2in)
2 gilt-plated earhooks

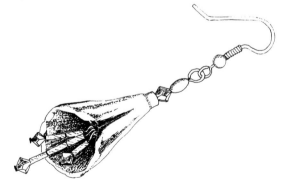

·*Multi-Drop with Faceted Beads*·

The main finding featured in these earrings is the multi-drop hanger. This one is very lightweight and not particularly strong, so I prefer to use two glued together back to back for each earring. Follow the order of threading beads shown in Fig 1.

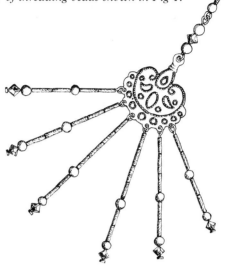

4 gilt-plated multi-drop hangers
14 AB coated faceted-crystal bicones, 3mm
26 gilt-plated metal beads, 3mm
60 gilt-plated heishi
14 gilt-plated headpins, 5cm (2in)
2 gilt-plated earhooks
Gel superglue (to glue the multi-drop hangers together)

Fig 1   Diagram to show order of threading

·*Stretched Spiral*·

The spiral wire used in this pair of earrings is the same as that used for the Peruvian Teardrop Earrings on pages 81–2. The only difference is that the spiral used here (below left) is slightly larger and has been stretched to accommodate the length of one headpin threaded with rocailles and metal beads. The earrings shown below right are similar, but with a smaller spiral and different beads threaded on to the headpin. To make these two pairs of earrings, follow the instructions for the Peruvian Teardrop Earrings.

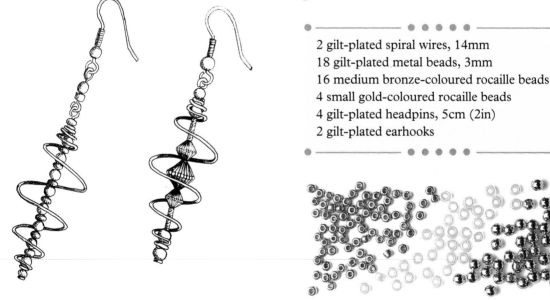

2 gilt-plated spiral wires, 14mm
18 gilt-plated metal beads, 3mm
16 medium bronze-coloured rocaille beads
4 small gold-coloured rocaille beads
4 gilt-plated headpins, 5cm (2in)
2 gilt-plated earhooks

·Rocaille Threaded Spiral·

Spiral wires again provide the base for these easily made, fun earrings. Here I have used ten shades of rocaille beads to give a graduation of colour, but you can change this to a single colour if preferred. Instructions for making up these earrings are given below.

2 gilt-plated spiral wires, 14mm
12 medium rocaille beads in each of
    10 different colours
6 gilt-plated heishi
2 gilt-plated metal beads, 3mm
2 gilt-plated fluted metal beads, 4 × 8mm
2 gilt-plated headpins, 5cm (2in)
2 gilt-plated jump rings
2 gilt-plated earhooks

1 Collect together all your beads and findings and place them in separate shallow containers on a tray.

2 Take one of the spirals, stretch it so that the middle coils remain open and, using cutting pliers, cut off the tightly coiled top of the open spiral (Fig 2).

3 Thread the rocaille beads, six of each colour at a time, on to this spiral in the required order.

4 When the beads have been threaded on there will be some spare exposed wire. Leaving enough to make a loop, cut this to size.

5 Make a loop in the top end of the spiral wire and attach one of the jump rings.

6 Thread the beads for the central hanger on to one of the headpins.

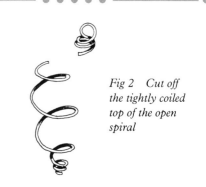

Fig 2   Cut off the tightly coiled top of the open spiral

7 Leaving enough to make a loop, cut off the spare headpin wire.

8 Make a loop in the headpin and attach it to the jump ring, so that the beaded headpin hangs inside the spiral.

9 Attach the earhook to the jump ring.

·*Rocaille Triangle*·

Rocailles are again the main beads used for these unusual earrings, which are very inexpensive to produce and can be made in almost any colour. Instructions are given below.

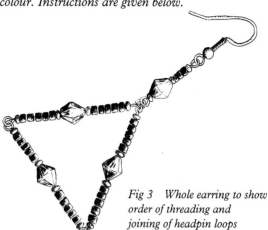

1 packet medium dark-mauve lustred rocaille beads
30 medium gold-coloured rocaille beads
8 dark mauve Indian glass lozenge beads, 8 × 10mm
8 gilt-plated headpins, 5cm (2in)
2 gilt-plated earhooks

Fig 3   Whole earring to show order of threading and joining of headpin loops

1 Collect together all your beads and findings and place them in separate shallow containers on a tray.
2 Cut the heads off all the headpins and make a loop at the end of one.
3 Attach this headpin loop to the earhook and thread on beads following the design from the photograph on page 109 and Fig 3. Cut off spare wire and make a loop.
4 Make a loop in the end of one of the other

headpins and attach it to the last loop made.
5 Thread beads on to this headpin following the design from the photograph and Fig 3. Make a loop in the end.
6 Repeat steps 4 and 5 with two more headpins, attaching the last loop made to the top loop of the first step 4 to form the triangle (Fig 3).

·*Triple Headpin Drop*·

These earrings are made using only the simple techniques of threading beads on to headpins, making loops in the headpins and attaching them to a jump ring, which in turn is attached to the earhook. Endless variations of this style can be made, and the design below right has been included in the photograph on page 109 as another idea which you may like to copy.

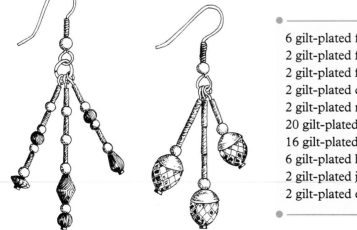

6 gilt-plated fluted beads, 4mm
2 gilt-plated fluted teardrops, 5 × 8mm
2 gilt-plated fluted bicones, 5 × 8mm
2 gilt-plated daisy-wheel beads, 8mm
2 gilt-plated metal beads, 3mm
20 gilt-plated metal beads, 2mm
16 gilt-plated heishi
6 gilt-plated headpins, 5cm (2in)
2 gilt-plated jump rings
2 gilt-plated earhooks

·Pink Teardrop with Filigree Cone·

I have made an exception here to my normal preference for no plastic, as although the teardrop bead is made from plastic it is so effective with this filigree cone that it deserves to be included. This teardrop is available in approximately twenty colours and the filigree cone is also made in a silver-plate finish. Making these earrings is very simple, but as the bead and cone together are too long for one headpin, instructions are given below to show you how to attach the earring to the earhook.

2 plastic teardrop beads, 10 × 35mm
2 gilt-plated filigree cones, 10 × 40mm
2 gilt-plated metal beads, 2mm
4 gilt-plated headpins, 5cm (2in)
2 gilt-plated earhooks

1 Collect together all your beads and findings and place them in separate shallow containers on a tray.
2 Take one headpin, thread on the teardrop bead, cut off spare headpin wire and make a loop close to the top of the bead.

3 Take another headpin, cut off the head and make a loop in one end. Attach this loop to the first one.
4 Thread on the cone and the gilt-plated metal bead.
5 Ensuring that the cone fits snugly on to the teardrop bead, cut off spare headpin wire and make a loop. Attach to the earhook.

· Rocaille Loops·

This earring is time-consuming to make as it involves threading so many small rocaille beads on to beading thread. However, once that is done the earrings can be completed quickly. As rocaille beads are available in a wide range of colours, you could make this style of earring to suit any occasion.

1 packet small rocaille beads
2 gilt-plated necklace end caps, 10mm
2 gilt-plated melon beads, 3 × 5mm
2 gilt-plated headpins, 5cm (2in)
2 gilt-plated earhooks
2 lengths woven-polyester beading thread,
each 56cm (22in)
Gel superglue
Liquid superglue

1 Collect together all your beads and findings and place them in separate shallow containers on a tray.

2 Following the instructions in Basic Necklace Threading on pages 19–20, prepare one of the lengths of polyester thread for threading.

3 Tie a spare bead loosely on to the other end of the thread and thread on 41cm (16in) of rocaille beads.

4 Remove the loosely tied bead and, allowing approximately 2cm (¾in) of spare thread, tie the two ends together. Dab a little superglue on to the knot and cut off the spare thread.

5 Following Fig 4a, make four equal-length loops of threaded rocaille beads.

6 Cut the head off one headpin and partially form a loop. With this loop, catch up all the threads at the top of the loops of rocaille (Fig 4b).

7 Close the headpin loop to secure the threads, and thread on the necklace end cap to cover the headpin loop and the top end of the loops of rocaille beads.

8 Thread on one rocaille bead, one gilt-plated

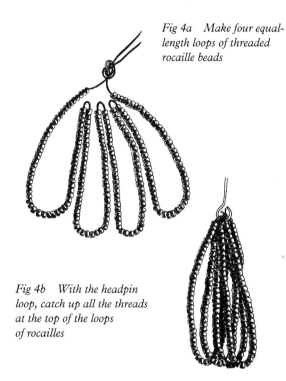

Fig 4a   Make four equal-length loops of threaded rocaille beads

Fig 4b   With the headpin loop, catch up all the threads at the top of the loops of rocailles

melon bead and one more rocaille bead.

9 Cut off spare headpin wire, form a loop and attach to the earhook.

·*Rainbow Fluorite and Flower Spacer*·

These earrings are made using sterling-silver spacers, and demonstrate the use of such findings in earring design. Many spacers of this type are available and the earrings below left show how you can even use simple curb chain as a 'spacer'. The method for making is very simple and requires only those techniques given in Basic Earring Making on page 21.

2 rainbow-fluorite beads, 10mm
2 sterling-silver flower spacers
2 sterling-silver headpins, 25mm (1in)
2 sterling-silver earhooks

· *MAKING YOUR OWN SIMPLE BEADS* ·

Making your own beads and producing jewellery from them can be very rewarding. Instructions are provided here for two different techniques which you can use at home to produce your own exclusive beads – no specialist tools are required. I also touch on the subject of ceramic beads and give you some ideas for making these for yourself.

· *Papier Mâché Beads* ·

Beads made from paper and glue can be surprisingly beautiful. The method described here turns a simple sheet of gift-wrapping paper into colourful barrel-shaped beads, and in the photograph on page 116 you will see necklaces made from examples of this type of bead. No instructions are given for these necklaces, as the beads you produce will be made from different wrapping paper and will therefore need other, complementary ready-made beads to enhance them.

1 sheet of gift-wrapping paper (must be porous)	Felt-tip pen, in a colour to match the gift-wrapping paper
Cold-water paste powder	Clear varnish or nail varnish
Plain wooden cocktail sticks	Fine bristle brush, for varnishing finished beads
Large scissors	Large household tray
Sandpaper, coarse and fine grain	Large potato

1 Following the directions on the packet, make up approximately two cups of the cold-water paste.

2 Cut the gift-wrapping paper into strips approximately 2.5 × 69cm (1 × 27in).

3 Take one of the strips of paper and immerse it in the paste.

4 When thoroughly soaked, wind the strip of paper tightly on to one of the cocktail sticks to form a firm barrel shape (Fig 1a). To make a neat and almost undetectable finish, tear across the end of the strip of paper before smoothing it on to the finished surface (Fig 1b).

5 Push one end of the cocktail stick into the potato, to hold the unfinished bead in a position where it can dry without touching anything else.

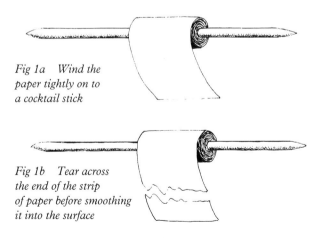

Fig 1a   Wind the paper tightly on to a cocktail stick

Fig 1b   Tear across the end of the strip of paper before smoothing it into the surface

6 After making up all the other beads in the same way, put your potato, which now looks like a colourful hedgehog, in a warm place for approximately 48 hours or until completely dry.

7 Remove the beads from the cocktail sticks by twisting them in the opposite direction to that in which the paper was wound on. This prevents any unravelling of the paper.

8 Smooth the ends of the beads by rubbing them first on the coarse and then on the fine sandpaper (Fig 2a).

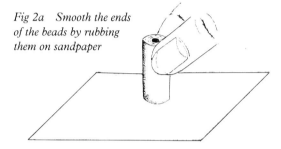

Fig 2a   Smooth the ends of the beads by rubbing them on sandpaper

9 These sanded ends will now appear white or at least paler than the rest of the bead. Disguise

this and any white paper showing along the torn edge of step 4 by colouring with the felt-tip pen (Fig 2b).

Fig 2b   Disguise the white paper showing at ends of the bead and along the tear by colouring with a matching felt-tip pen

10 One by one, put the beads back on to the cocktail sticks and give them a light coating of varnish. Try not to touch the cocktail sticks with the varnish as this could make removal of the beads a little difficult. As in step 5, support the beads in the potato for drying.

11 When the varnish is dry, remove the beads from the cocktail sticks. They are now ready for threading.

· *Polymer 'Clay' Beads* ·

Polymer 'clay' can be used to make beads in almost as many variations of style as traditionally made glass or ceramic beads. The range of colours available is vast and the design possibilities are limited only by your imagination. The two styles of bead described here can be adapted and elaborated upon to produce stunning beads of your own colour choice and pattern. The actual instructions given are for the beads used in the necklaces shown in the photographs on pages 116 and 120.

· *Grey-Green with White Swirls* ·

These beads are made from just three colours of Fimo modelling material (you may be using a different make and if so should keep the proportion of clay used the same as shown here), and the simple method provides an easy introduction to polymer-'clay' modelling. Beads produced in this style are very useful and attractive for bead jewellery, especially when, as here, some of the colours used have a metallic finish.

The ingredients and instructions given below will make approximately forty 12mm beads. The measure of a 'block' refers to half of a 65gm (2¼oz) packet of Fimo.

1 block each metallic polymer 'clay' in grey
and dark green
½ block white polymer 'clay'
Small sharp knife

Darning needle or hatpin
Household tray (to work on)
Baking tray

1 Straight from the packet, polymer 'clay' is quite hard and not easily worked in large quantities, so you will need to divide the amounts given above into smaller pieces. When dividing the 'clay', be sure to keep the proportions to be worked together the same as in the list of ingredients, ie one of white to two of the other colours. To do this, mark out your blocks of 'clay' into equal portions using a small knife (Fig 3). The shaded portions show a suitable amount with which to work and will make ten beads.

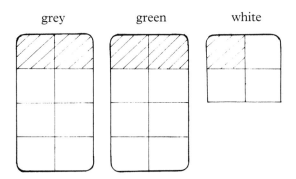

grey   green   white

Fig 3   Blocks of polymer 'clay' marked to allow for easy division, keeping the proportions correct for working

2 Take one portion of white 'clay' and soften it by kneading in your hands. Do not be put off by it appearing at first to have a crumbly texture – this soon disappears and the material will become soft, smooth and pliable.
3 When this stage has been reached roll the 'clay' into a round strip approximately 15cm (6in) long.
4 Repeat steps 2 and 3 with the other two

colours and lay all the colours down together (Fig 4).

white

green   grey

Fig 4   Three strips of colour positioned as in step 4

5 Roll all the colours together to make one long, round strip, twist it and then fold it double.
6 Roll the two strips together and when smooth, again twist and fold double. Keep repeating this process until the strips of colour are mingled together to your satisfaction.
7 At this stage you will have one smooth, round strip of 'clay' with the colours all in fairly fine stripes. Lay this on a tray, or other suitable cutting surface, and divide it into ten equal portions, using a small knife (Fig 5).
8 Take one of these portions and roll it gently in the palms of your hands to form a sphere.
9 Using the darning needle or hatpin, make a hole through the centre of this sphere to turn it into a bead. You will find that pushing the needle through will distort the shape a little, but this can be corrected easily by rolling it very gently in your hand.
10 Repeat steps 8 and 9 to make all the beads from the prepared 'clay'.
11 Repeat steps 2–10 with the rest of the 'clay'.
12 Place all the still soft beads on a clean baking tray (being careful not to distort them or allow them to touch each other) and, following the polymer 'clay' manufacturer's instructions, place them in a warm oven to harden. The beads are then ready for use.

Fig 5   The finished strip of clay with colours well mingled. Divide into ten equal portions

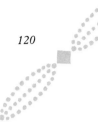

· *Brown and Millefiori* ·

These beads are made using similar techniques to those employed in the manufacture of glass millefiori. The 'cane' used here is very simple to make and can be produced easily by complete beginners.

The ingredients and instructions given below will make approximately sixteen 12mm beads, or enough beads of varying sizes to make the graduated necklace shown below. The measure of a 'block' refers to half of a 65gm (2¼oz) packet of Fimo polymer 'clay'.

1 block metallic-brown polymer 'clay' ⅛ block of polymer 'clay' in beige, yellow, red and plain brown (you will not use up all of these quantities)	Small fine, sharp knife Darning needle or hatpin Household tray (to work on) Baking tray

1 Take a small portion of the red polymer 'clay' and, as in step 2 of the previous project, knead it until it is soft.

2 Roll this into a round strip approximately 4mm (⅙in) in diameter and 8cm (3in) long.

3 Take a small portion of the yellow 'clay', knead it until soft and roll it into five round strips of approximately 2mm (¹⁄₁₂in) in diameter and 8cm (3in) long.

4 Following Fig 6a, apply the yellow strips at even intervals along the length of the red strip. The softened material sticks easily together.

5 Take a small portion of the plain brown 'clay' and repeat step 3.

Fig 6a Apply the yellow strips of 'clay' at even intervals along the length of the red strip in the centre

6 Following Fig 6b, apply the brown strips to the gaps left between the yellow strips.

Fig 6b   Apply the brown strips to the gaps between the yellow strips

7 Take a small piece of the beige 'clay', knead it until soft and then flatten it to a thin rectangle large enough to wrap around all the other strips of prepared 'clays' (Fig 6c). This is your millefiori 'cane'.

Fig 6c   Wrap the beige 'clay' around all the other prepared strips

8 Roll the cane until smooth, thinner and approximately 10cm (4in) long. Using a fine, sharp knife, trim the ends to reveal the pattern, which should look like Fig 6d.

Fig 6d   The finished 'cane'

9 Divide the metallic-brown 'clay' into bead-sized portions – see Fig 7, which allows for making sixteen beads of a regular 12mm size.
10 Take one of these portions, knead it until soft and smooth and then form it into a sphere.
11 With the sharp knife, cut off a very fine slice

of the 'cane' and place it on the surface of the sphere (it will stick easily). Repeat this process until you have as much millefiori decoration as you require (Fig 8).

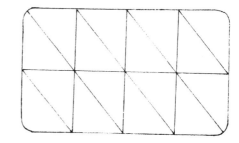

Fig 7   Block of polymer 'clay' marked out for making sixteen 12mm beads

Fig 8   Apply slices of millefiori cane to the surface of the sphere

12 Take the sphere in your hands and roll it gently in your palms until the millefiori decoration is smoothed into the surface.
13 Using the darning needle or hatpin, make a hole through the centre of the sphere to turn it into a bead. Correct any distortion caused in making the hole by gently rolling the bead in your hands.
14 Repeat steps 10–13 with the rest of the metallic-brown 'clay'.
15 Place all the still soft beads on a clean baking tray (being careful not to distort them or allow them to touch each other) and, following the polymer 'clay' manufacturer's instructions, place them in a warm oven to harden. The beads are then ready for use.

·*Ceramic and Air-Drying Clay Beads*·

If you have access to a kiln you may like to try making your own ceramic beads. As an alternative to real clay there are some quite good air-drying 'clay' materials and after firing, or drying, the appearance of both is quite similar. In the photograph below, the beads on the leather thong are made from a real terracotta clay, while those with the painted decoration are made from air-drying 'clay'.

There are three ways in which real clay beads may be decorated: a pattern can be impressed into the surface, they can be painted or they can be glazed. Only the first two methods apply to the air-drying 'clay', though that too can be given a glazed appearance with the use of varnish.

Precise instructions are not given here, as the method for forming a bead is simply to roll a piece of clay in your hands to form a sphere and then, as in step 13 of the previous project, to make a hole through it using a darning needle or hatpin. The decoration of your beads will be totally individual – whether pressed pattern, painted or glazed – and only experiment and practice will achieve results with which you are happy.

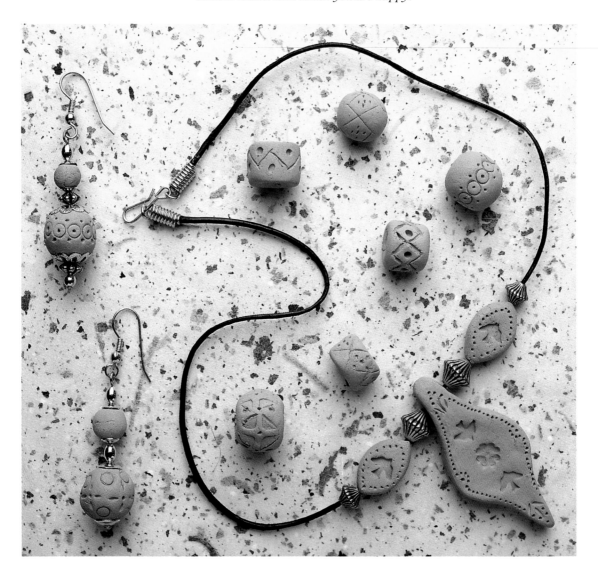

The following pages are for quick reference. They give brief descriptions and explanations of some of the unfamiliar words and terms used in this book.

AB COATING   Short for aurora borealis, AB refers to a surface coating applied to some beads to give a special iridescent finish.

ALPHABET BEAD   Small beads, usually glass, with single letters of the alphabet on each.

AMETHYST   Semi-precious stone in varying shades of mauve, clear or semi-transparent.

BARREL BEAD   The name given to barrel-shaped beads.

BARREL CLASP   Barrel-shaped clasp which is secured by a central screw. See photograph on page 15.

BEAD CAP   Small finding, usually metal, used at either end of some beads either for design purposes or to stop headpins or small beads pulling through larger-holed beads. See photograph on page 15.

BEAD TASSEL   Several beaded threads, usually rocailles, hanging together. Useful hanging beneath a single pendant bead.

BEADING NEEDLE   Very fine version of sewing needle.

BEADING TRAY   Purpose-made tray especially for necklace design and threading. See photograph on pages 8–9.

BICONE   Bead in which both ends are cone shaped.

BIWA PEARL   Name often given to freshwater pearls as in the past many came from Lake Biwa in Japan.

BOLT-RING CLASP   A round, open clasp which operates like a door bolt but with a tiny internal spring to keep the bolt closed. See photograph on page 15.

BOX CLASP   General term used to describe clasps in which a hook fastening is hidden beneath a fancy hollow exterior. See photograph on page 15.

BUGLE BEAD   Small tube-shaped glass bead varying in length from 2mm to 25mm. See page 10.

CALOTTE   Metal finding used in necklace making to cover the finishing knots and provide a fixing point for the clasp. See photograph on page 15.

CANE   Name given to the rods of glass from which beads are made. These may be of a single colour, decorated with stripes or more elaborately formed into millefiori (see below).

CARNELIAN   Semi-precious stone, occurring in varied shades of translucent amber through to a dark reddish-brown. Also known as cornelian.

CERAMIC   General word for all fired-clay products.

CHOKER   Short-length necklace which fits on or just below the neck.

CINNABAR   Material derived from sulphide of mercury used, in China, to make moulded and carved beads.

CLOISONNÉ   Literally this means enclosures or partitions. In beading terms it refers to beautifully enamelled beads, where the decorative enamelled colours are separated by fine wire soldered to a brass base-bead.

CLUTCH Earstud-back, usually round type, also sometimes used as the name for a scroll-type earstud-back.

CRIMP Metal finding used in necklace making to secure thread or leather thong by being squeezed tight over the threading material. See photograph on page 15.

CRUMB BEAD Bead on which the surface decoration has been applied by rolling the still soft bead in granules of coloured glass.

CRYSTAL Clear glass-like, semi-precious stone or a bright, clear glass. In bead making both are usually facet cut to give brilliant sparkle.

CUSHION Round bead flattened from pole to pole.

DAISY-WHEEL BEAD My name for the small daisy-shaped cushion bead used in many of the designs in this book.

DECAL Type of decoration applied by transfer.

DISC Not a record, but term used to describe a bead of similar shape, ie flat with a central hole.

EARCLIP Earring fitting for unpierced ears. Fits to the ear with a spring closing clip.

EARHOOK General term given to an earfitting that is worn by hooking through the ear. Specific names include fishhook, ball-and-spring or shepherd's crook.

EARPOST General term given to an earfitting with a straight wire to pass through the ear which is secured by a scroll (or clutch, see above) at the back of the ear.

EBONY A very dark, usually almost black, wood often used for bead making.

EMBROIDERY STONE Flat-backed glass shape often faceted and with holes for sewing to fabrics. Can also be incorporated into bead jewellery (see Amber Teardrop on page 46).

ENAMEL Coloured clear or opaque glass substance fused to the surface of metal by heating in a kiln.

FACETED BEAD Bead with machine-cut surfaces to provide flat planes which reflect light.

FAIENCE BEAD Small, early (from approximately 4000BC) mass-produced bead with a fine glaze, round or tubular in shape, usually blue in colour but sometimes green or white. See page 6.

FEATHERING Decorative technique used on glass beads in which a sharp instrument is used to drag out threads of colour across the surface of the semi-molten bead.

FEATURE BEAD The dominant, or special, beads in a necklace design.

FILIGREE Delicate metalwork used in some beads and findings.

FILLER BEAD Inexpensive, usually mass-produced bead, especially useful in necklace making.

FINDINGS General term given to the components such as clasps and earhooks that are necessary for the completion of bead jewellery. See photograph on page 15.

FLUTED Longitudinal grooved finish often applied to metal beads.

FOB CLASP Metal clasp consisting of two parts, one a T-bar and the other a circle through which the T-bar fits. See photograph on page 15.

FOILED LAMP BEAD Bead in which a reflective sparkle is achieved by the insertion of metallic foil under the surface of the glass during manufacture.

FOSSIL STONE Type of limestone often dyed to brilliant colours and used for bead making.

FRESHWATER PEARL Unevenly shaped, often oval, pearl produced by freshwater mussels, often also known as Biwa pearl (see above). Many are now cultivated in China.

FROSTED GLASS Finish which can be applied to beads by tumbling in abrasive grits after manufacture.

GARNET Semi-precious stone, a beautiful clear, deep red.

GLAZE Fine glass coating applied by firing in a kiln. Used for faience beads, porcelain and some clay beads.

GOLDSTONE Type of glass used in bead making which is given a glittering sparkle by inclusion of tiny fragments of copper filings during manufacture.

HAEMATITE Very heavy semi-precious stone, an iron ore which can be cut and polished to a very shiny mirror-like black finish.

HATPIN Long pointed headpin for threading beads to make a decorative hatpin or lapel pin.

HEADPIN Length of hard wire, in a large range of sizes, with a head like a dressmaker's pin. Used for suspending beads, particularly in earring making.

HEISHI Small tube-shaped metal bead.

HOGAN BEAD Term used to describe fluted metal bicone beads.

HOOK CLASP Simple metal clasp which fastens by hooking into a jump ring or loop.

HOWLITE Natural stone occurring in white with grey marbling, often dyed to imitate semi-precious stones such as turquoise or lapis lazuli.

HYBRID FINDINGS Findings which combine different metals in their make-up, eg a stud-type earring fitting may have a stainless steel post and a gilt-plated ball to overcome metal allergy problems. See photograph on page 17.

INLAY   Form of decoration used on some beads where substances such as mother-of-pearl or brass wire are inserted into the surface. Most often used on wooden or horn beads.

JET   Very hard form of lignite (fossilised wood and vegetation) which is black and will take a polish to become very shiny. Used to make beads and other jewellery, especially in Victorian times when it became very popular for wear during mourning.

JUMP RING   Metal finding, ring shaped and used in jewellery making to join one thing to another. See photograph on page 17.

KILN BEADS   Glass bead whose heat source for manufacture is provided by a kiln.

KNOTTED NECKLACE   Necklace with a knot tied between each bead.

LAC BEAD   Bead made from the resinous substance produced by some trees in which the lac beetle lives.

LAMP BEAD   Glass bead handmade using the intense heat produced by a 'lamp' to melt the glass cane.

LAPIS LAZULI   Semi-precious stone, prized since the early Egyptian times for its lovely opaque, rich blue colour.

LEATHER THONG   Round lengths of leather in varying thicknesses useful for some styles of necklace threading.

LEOPARDSKIN RHYOLITE   Unusual stone occurring in varied shades of brown, black and grey. The name must be derived from its blotchy, spotted appearance which resembles the coat of a leopard.

MALACHITE   Semi-precious stone, in a rich, banded, opaque green colour.

MELON   Term used to describe oval-shaped beads.

METALLISED   Term used to describe a bead or finding made from plastic but given a surface coating or appearance of metal.

MILLEFIORI   Literally 'thousand flowers'. A type of decoration applied to a plain glass bead-base by surface application of sections of flower-patterned glass cane. The technique for making the cane can now be imitated in bead making with polymer clays. See Do It Yourself, pages 120–1.

MIRACLE BEAD   Plastic bead given a glowing lustre by the inclusion of a metallic layer just beneath the surface.

MONOFILAMENT NYLON   The same material as fishing line. Best used for catching fish!

MOSS AGATE   Semi-precious stone; semi-transparent greyish base colour with lots of green moss-like inclusions.

NECKLACE END CAP   Metal bell-shaped finding used at either end of some necklaces, especially where it is desirable to hide the end beads. Particularly useful in multi-stranded necklaces. See photograph on page 15.

NYLON-COATED WIRE   Also known as tiger tail. A fine multi-stranded twisted wire covered with nylon. Very strong and useful for threading heavy, sharp-edged beads.

OBSIDIAN MAHOGANY   Natural stone of volcanic origin, mainly brown in colour, occasionally with some black.

PAPIER MÂCHÉ   Hard substance made by combining paper and glue. Can be used to make beads. See pages 116–18.

PEARL   Much-valued gem produced by oysters, clams or mussels when they secrete calcium carbonate in response to irritation under the shell, caused by a small invading particle such as sand. Also used to describe imitation pearls.

PLIERS   Gripping tool in various styles, each suited to particular jobs.

PLIERS, CUTTING   Used for cutting wire. See photograph on pages 8–9.

PLIERS, FLAT-NOSED   Used for bending wire and opening and closing loops and jump rings. See photograph on pages 8–9.

PLIERS, HOUSEHOLD   General craft-type pliers which incorporate the features of flat-nosed and cutting pliers.

PLIERS, ROUND-NOSED   Used for bending wire into round loops. See photograph on pages 8–9.

PORCELAIN   Very fine ceramic material used by the Chinese to produce beautiful beads.

RAINBOW FLUORITE   Semi-precious stone occurring in many shades from clear pale green through to deepest purple, and often in bands of several colours close together. A soft stone which needs to be treated with care.

RELEASE AGENT   Term used to describe the material applied to the metal rod on which glass beads are made to facilitate their removal when completed.

ROCAILLE BEAD   Small glass bead, 2mm to 5mm, made in a multitude of colours. Often referred to as seed or love beads.

ROCAILLE, SILVER-LINED   Clear-glass rocaille bead given extra sparkle by a silver lining to the hole.

ROSEWOOD   Hard, dark wood, usually reddish in colour and supposedly with a rose-like scent.

SCOTCH PIN   Similar to a kilt-fastening pin. When used as a bead finding it is originally straight to allow for threading on of beads. See photograph on page 17.

SHORTENER CLASP   Oval clasp with a central hinge which allows it to open for use with long necklaces so that they may be twisted and worn double, with the clasp securing the two looped ends. See photograph on page 15.

SIEVE BROOCH-BACK   Metal finding in which the base of the brooch is perforated to allow the 'sewing' on of beads. See photograph on page 17.

SPACER   Decorative link between beads, usually metal. See photograph on page 15.

SPACER BAR   Bar, usually made of metal, with two or more holes through from side to side. Used in some styles of necklace to hold strands of beads in position. See Cretan Memories photograph on page 77.

SPIRAL WIRES   Preformed spirals of wire with tight coils top and bottom. See photograph on page 17.

SPLIT RING   Metal finding, often used for keyrings but also made in small 6mm sizes which are useful for providing a fastening for trigger or bolt-ring clasps. See photograph on page 17.

SUPERGLUE, GEL   Cyanoacrylate glue in gel form. More controllable than liquid superglue and therefore useful for applying the small amounts necessary to secure knots in necklace making.

SUPERGLUE, LIQUID   Cyanoacrylate glue in liquid form, useful to stiffen the threading end of beading thread so that it can be used without a needle. See pages 19–20.

When using this glue please heed all warnings on the product packaging as superglue bonds to skin in seconds.

SUPERGLUE RELEASE AGENT   For use when you have not heeded the warnings mentioned above! An 'oily' substance which slowly dissolves superglue.

TEARDROP   Bead shape in which one end of the bead is larger than the other. Also sometimes described as pear shaped.

TERRACOTTA   Natural reddish-brown clay.

TIGER EYE   Semi-precious stone, opaque golden-brown with striated markings.

TRADE BEAD   Bead used worldwide for trading purposes.

TRIGGER CLASP   Open clasp which has a spring opening mechanism. See photograph on page 15.

TWISTED-WIRE BEADING 'NEEDLE'   Fine pliable 'needle' made from a twisted length of extremely small-gauge wire.

WORRY BEADS   String of sixteen beads, with tied ends of thread finished with a tassel. Any type of bead may be used. Seen particularly in Greece.

ACKNOWLEDGEMENTS

Where do I begin? Nearly everyone around me has been affected in some way by the writing of this book, from my friends and family, whose company I have missed, to my children who have learned how to cook in this last six months! First and foremost I must thank my husband David, without whose humour, understanding and encouragement this book would never have been written. My children, Andrew and Theresa, also deserve special mention as they have put up with a preoccupied Mum whose main cooking attempts lately seem to have consisted of oven-ready fast food. I promise to do better in the near future!

My thanks also go to my friend Jill Harris and her daughter Julie; Jill for her assistance in my business and for making up some of the jewellery contained within these pages, and Julie for her introduction to my patient editor Vivienne Wells. I am grateful also to Bill and Martin Tuffnell, who gave me a whole day of their time to explain the intricacies of glass lamp-bead making.

Last but not least, I would like to thank another friend, Evelyn Bartlett, for her detailed and delightful paintings which really show off these beautiful beads.

SUPPLIERS

Thousands of different beads and findings, including most of those shown within *Making Beaded Jewellery*, are available from the extensive Bead Exclusive catalogue where Barbara has had her projects packed in kit form ready for you to make into your own stunning jewellery. For a copy of this exciting colour catalogue contact:

Bead Exclusive
4 Samara Business Park
Cavalier Road
Heathfield
Newton Abbot
Devon TQ12 6TR

Tel: 01626 834934   Fax: 01626 834787
E-mail: bead.exclusive@virgin.net

UK

Martin Tuffnell
Unit 8 EWBC
Nursery Units
Kellythorpe Industrial
    Estate
Kellythorpe
Nr Driffield
East Yorkshire

The London Bead Co
25 Chalk Farm Rd
Camden Town
London
NW1 8AG

S. Tomalin
259 Portobello Rd
London
W11 1LR

The Polyclay Studio
14 Barrington Rd
Horsham
West Sussex
RH13 5SN

Spangles
1 Casburn Lane
Burwell
Cambridgeshire
CB5 0ED

The Bead Shop
43 Neal Street
Covent Garden
WC2H 9PJ

Ells and Farrier Ltd
Denmark Works
Sheepcote
Dell Rd
Beamond End
Amersham
Buckinghamshire
HP7 0RX

Rocking Rabbit
Market Street
Newmarket
Suffolk
CB8 8EE

CANADA

Beadbox
1234 Robson St
Vancouver
BC V6E 1C1

USA

Beadworks
139 Washington St
South Norwalk
CT 06854

Beadworks
905 South Ann St
Baltimore
MD21231

Beadworks
23 Church St
Cambridge
Mass 02318

Beadworks
1420 Avenue K
Plano
Dallas
Texas 75074

Beadworks
68 Greenwich Avenue
Greenwich
CT 06830

Beadworks
349 Newbury St
Boston
Mass 02115

Beadworks
225 South St
Philadelphia
PA 19147

Beadworks
227 Goddard Row
Brickmarket
Newport
RI 02840

Beadworks
Stockyards Station
140 East Exchange
    Avenue
Fort Worth
Texas 76106

FRANCE

Le Comptoir Des Perles
17 rue de la Republique
F-78100 Saint
    Germain en Laye

GERMANY

Perlenmarkt
Nordenstrasse 28
8000 Munchen 40

Perlenmarkt
Kaustrasse 93
1000 Berlin 12

Perlenmarkt
Bohlenplatz 12
8520 Erlangen

Perlenmarkt
Alte Gasse 14/16
6000 Frankfurt 1

Perlenmarkt
Albrecht Durer
    Strasse 16
8500 Nurnburg

Knopf and Perle
Kornhaus Platz 2
7900 Ulm

Perlplex
Guntramstrasse 58
7800 Frieburg

INDEX